Python for Secret Agents
Volume II

Gather, analyze, and decode data to reveal hidden facts using Python, the perfect tool for all aspiring secret agents

Steven F. Lott

BIRMINGHAM - MUMBAI

Python for Secret Agents
Volume II

Copyright © 2015 Packt Publishing

All rights reserved. No part of this book may be reproduced, stored in a retrieval system, or transmitted in any form or by any means, without the prior written permission of the publisher, except in the case of brief quotations embedded in critical articles or reviews.

Every effort has been made in the preparation of this book to ensure the accuracy of the information presented. However, the information contained in this book is sold without warranty, either express or implied. Neither the author,nor Packt Publishing, and its dealers and distributors will be held liable for any damages caused or alleged to be caused directly or indirectly by this book.

Packt Publishing has endeavored to provide trademark information about all of the companies and products mentioned in this book by the appropriate use of capitals. However, Packt Publishing cannot guarantee the accuracy of this information.

First published: August 2014

Second edition: December 2015

Production reference: 2111215

Published by Packt Publishing Ltd.
Livery Place
35 Livery Street
Birmingham B3 2PB, UK.

ISBN 978-1-78528-340-6

www.packtpub.com

Credits

Author
Steven F. Lott

Reviewer
Shubham Sharma

Commissioning Editor
Julian Ursell

Acquisition Editors
Subho Gupta

Sam Wood

Content Development Editor
Riddhi Tuljapurkar

Technical Editor
Danish Shaikh

Copy Editor
Vibha Shukla

Project Coordinator
Sanchita Mandal

Proofreader
Safis Editing

Indexer
Priya Sane

Graphics
Kirk D'Penha

Production Coordinator
Komal Ramchandani

Cover Work
Komal Ramchandani

About the Author

Steven F. Lott has been programming since the 70s, when computers were large, expensive, and rare. As a contract software developer and architect, he has worked on hundreds of projects from very small to very large. He's been using Python to solve business problems for over 10 years.

He's currently leveraging Python to implement microservices and ETL pipelines.

His other titles with Packt Publishing include *Python Essentials*, *Mastering Object-Oriented Python*, *Functional Python Programming*, and *Python for Secret Agents*.

Steven is currently a technomad who lives in various places on the East Coast of the U.S. His technology blog is `http://slott-softwarearchitect.blogspot.com`.

About the Reviewer

Shubham Sharma holds a bachelor's degree in computer science engineering with specialization in business analytics and optimization from UPES, Dehradun. He has a good skill set of programming languages. He also has an experience in web development ,Android, and ERP development and works as a freelancer.

Shubham also loves writing and blogs at `www.cyberzonec.in/blog`. He is currently working on Python for the optimal specifications and identifications of mobile phones from customer reviews.

www.PacktPub.com

Support files, eBooks, discount offers, and more

For support files and downloads related to your book, please visit www.PacktPub.com.

Did you know that Packt offers eBook versions of every book published, with PDF and ePub files available? You can upgrade to the eBook version at www.PacktPub.com and as a print book customer, you are entitled to a discount on the eBook copy. Get in touch with us at service@packtpub.com for more details.

At www.PacktPub.com, you can also read a collection of free technical articles, sign up for a range of free newsletters and receive exclusive discounts and offers on Packt books and eBooks.

https://www2.packtpub.com/books/subscription/packtlib

Do you need instant solutions to your IT questions? PacktLib is Packt's online digital book library. Here, you can search, access, and readPackt's entire library of books.

Why subscribe?

- Fully searchable across every book published by Packt
- Copy and paste, print, and bookmark content
- On demand and accessible via a web browser

Free access for Packt account holders

If you have an account with Packt at www.PacktPub.com, you can use this to access PacktLib today and view 9 entirely free books. Simply use your login credentials for immediate access.

Table of Contents

Preface	**v**
Chapter 1: New Missions – New Tools	**1**
Background briefing on tools	**2**
Doing a Python upgrade	3
Preliminary mission to upgrade pip	5
Background briefing: review of the Python language	**6**
Using variables to save results	7
Using the sequence collections: strings	8
Using other common sequences: tuples and lists	11
Using the dictionary mapping	12
Comparing data and using the logic operators	13
Using some simple statements	14
Using compound statements for conditions: if	15
Using compound statements for repetition: for and while	16
Defining functions	17
Creating script files	18
Mission One – upgrade Beautiful Soup	**20**
Getting an HTML page	21
Navigating the HTML structure	22
Doing other upgrades	**24**
Mission to expand our toolkit	**25**
Scraping data from PDF files	26
Sidebar on the ply package	28
Building our own gadgets	28
Getting the Arduino IDE	29
Getting a Python serial interface	31
Summary	**32**

Table of Contents

Chapter 2: Tracks, Trails, and Logs — 33

Background briefing – web servers and logs — 34
Understanding the variety of formats — 34
Getting a web server log — 35

Writing a regular expression for parsing — 35
Introducing some regular expression rules and patterns — 37
Finding a pattern in a file — 38
Using regular expression suffix operators — 41
Capturing characters by name — 43
Looking at the CLF — 44

Reading and understanding the raw data — 47
Reading a gzip compressed file — 48

Reading remote files — 50
Studying a log in more detail — 50
What are they downloading? — 52
Trails of activity — 53
Who is this person? — 55
Using Python to run other programs — 56
Processing whois queries — 57
Breaking a request into stanzas and lines — 58
Alternate stanza-finding algorithm — 60
Making bulk requests — 60

Getting logs from a server with ftplib — 61
Building a more complete solution — 62

Summary — 63

Chapter 3: Following the Social Network — 65

Background briefing – images and social media — 66
Accessing web services with urllib or http.client — 68

Who's doing the talking? — 71
Starting with someone we know — 74
Finding our followers — 76

What do they seem to be talking about? — 79
What are they posting? — 81
Deep Under Cover – NLTK and language analysis — 83
Summary — 85

Table of Contents

Chapter 4: Dredging up History — 87

Background briefing–Portable Document Format — **88**

Extracting PDF content — **90**

Using generator expressions — 90

Writing generator functions — 92

Filtering bad data — 93

Writing a context manager — 94

Writing a PDF parser resource manager — 96

Extending the resource manager — 97

Getting text data from a document — **100**

Displaying blocks of text — 101

Understanding tables and complex layouts — **103**

Writing a content filter — 105

Filtering the page iterator — 107

Exposing the grid — 108

Making some text block recognition tweaks — 110

Emitting CSV output — 111

Summary — **112**

Chapter 5: Data Collection Gadgets — 115

Background briefing: Arduino basics — **116**

Organizing a shopping list — 118

Getting it right the first time — 118

Starting with the digital output pins — **119**

Designing an external LED — 121

Assembling a working prototype — 124

Mastering the Arduino programming language — **126**

Using the arithmetic and comparison operators — 127

Using common processing statements — 128

Hacking and the edit, download, test and break cycle — 130

Seeing a better blinking light — **130**

Simple Arduino sensor data feed — **132**

Collecting analog data — **135**

Collecting bulk data with the Arduino — **138**

Controlling data collection — 140

Table of Contents

Data modeling and analysis with Python   **141**
Collecting data from the serial port   142
Formatting the collected data   143
Crunching the numbers   145
Creating a linear model   147
Reducing noise with a simple filter   **150**
Solving problems adding an audible alarm   **153**
Summary   **154**
Index   **157**

Preface

Secret agents are dealers and brokers of information. Information that's rare or difficult to acquire has the most value. Getting, analyzing, and sharing this kind of intelligence requires a skilled use of specialized tools. This often includes programming languages such as Python and its vast ecosystem of add-on libraries.

The best agents keep their toolkits up to date. This means downloading and installing the very latest in updated software. An agent should be able to analyze logs and other large sets of data to locate patterns and trends. Social network applications such as Twitter can reveal a great deal of useful information.

An agent shouldn't find themselves stopped by arcane or complex document formats. With some effort, the data in a PDF file can be as accessible as the data in a plain text file. In some cases, agents need to build specialized devices to gather data. A small processing such as an Arduino can gather raw data for analysis and dissemination; it moves the agent to the Internet of Things.

What this book covers

Chapter 1, *New Missions – New Tools*, addresses the tools that we're going to use. It's imperative that agents use the latest and most sophisticated tools. We'll guide field agents through the procedures required to get Python 3.4. We'll install the Beautiful Soup package, which helps you analyze and extract data from HTML pages. We'll install the Twitter API so that we can extract data from the social network. We'll add PDFMiner3K so that we can dig data out of PDF files. We'll also add the Arduino IDE so that we can create customized gadgets based on the Arduino processor.

Preface

Chapter 2, Tracks, Trails, and Logs, looks at the analysis of bulk data. We'll focus on the kinds of logs produced by web servers as they have an interesting level of complexity and contain valuable information on who's providing intelligence data and who's gathering this data. We'll leverage Python's regular expression module, re, to parse log data files. We'll also look at ways in which we can process compressed files using the gzip module.

Chapter 3, Following the Social Network, discusses one of the social networks. A field agent should know who's communicating and what they're communicating about. A network such as Twitter will reveal social connections based on who's following whom. We can also extract meaningful content from a Twitter stream, including text and images.

Chapter 4, Dredging Up History, provides you with essential pointers on extracting useful data from PDF files. Many agents find that a PDF file is a kind of dead-end because the data is inaccessible. There are tools that allow us to extract useful data from PDF. As PDF is focused on high-quality printing and display, it can be challenging to extract data suitable for analysis. We'll show some techniques with the PDFMiner package that can yield useful intelligence. Our goal is to transform a complex file into a simple CSV file, very much similar to the logs that we analyzed in *Chapter 2, Tracks, Trails, and Logs.*

Chapter 5, Data Collection Gadgets, expands the field agent's scope of operations to the Internet of Things (IoT). We'll look at ways to create simple Arduino sketches in order to read a typical device; in this case, an infrared distance sensor. We'll look at how we will gather and analyze raw data to do instrument calibration.

What you need for this book

A field agent needs a computer over which they have administrative privileges. We'll be installing additional software. A secret agent without the administrative password may have trouble installing Python 3 or any of the additional packages that we'll be using.

For agents using Windows, most of the packages will come prebuilt using the .EXE installers.

For agents using Linux, developer's tools are required. The complete suite of developer's tools is generally needed. The Gnu C Compiler (GCC) is the backbone of these tools.

For agents using Mac OS X, the developer's tool, XCode, is required and can be found at `https://developer.apple.com/xcode/`. We'll also need to install a tool called **homebrew** (`http://brew.sh`) to help us add Linux packages to Mac OS X.

Python 3 is available from the Python download page at `https://www.python.org/download`.

We'll download and install several things beyond Python 3.4 itself:

- The **Pillow** package will allow us to work with image files: `https://pypi.python.org/pypi/Pillow/2.4.0`
- The Beautiful Soup version 4 package will allow us to work with HTML web pages: `https://pypi.python.org/pypi/beautifulsoup4/4.3.2`
- The Twitter API package will let us search the social network: `https://pypi.python.org/pypi/TwitterAPI/2.3.3`
- We'll use PDF Miner 3k to extract meaningful data from PDF files: `https://pypi.python.org/pypi/pdfminer3k/1.3.0`
- We'll use the Arduino IDE. This comes from `https://www.arduino.cc/en/Main/Software`. We'll also want to install PySerial: `https://pypi.python.org/pypi/pyserial/2.7`
- This should demonstrate how extensible Python is. Almost anything an agent might need is already be written and available through the Python Package Index (PyPi) at `https://pypi.python.org/pypi`.

Who this book is for

This book is for field agents who know a little bit of Python and are very comfortable installing new software. Agents must be ready, willing, and able to write some new and clever programs in Python. An agent who has never done any programming before may find some of this a bit advanced; a beginner's tutorial in the basics of Python may be helpful as preparation.

We'll expect that an agent using this book is comfortable with simple mathematics. This involves some basic statistics and elementary geometry.

We expect that secret agents using this book will be doing their own investigations as well. The book's examples are designed to get the agent started down the road to develop interesting and useful applications. Each agent will have to explore further afield on their own.

Preface

Conventions

In this book, you will find a number of text styles that distinguish between different kinds of information. Here are some examples of these styles and an explanation of their meaning.

Code words in text, package names, folder names, filenames, file extensions, pathnames, dummy URLs, user input, and Twitter handles are shown as follows: "We can include other contexts through the use of the `include` directive."

A block of code is set as follows:

```
from fractions import Fraction
p = 0
for i in range(1, 2000):
    p += Fraction(1, i**2)
print( (p*6)**Fraction(1/2) )
```

When we wish to draw your attention to a particular part of a code block, the relevant lines or items are set in bold:

```
from fractions import Fraction
p = 0
for i in range(1, 2000):
    p += Fraction(1, i**2)
print( (p*6)**Fraction(1/2) )
```

Any command-line input or output is written as follows:

```
$ python3.4 -m doctest ourfile.py
```

New terms and **important words** are shown in bold. Words that you see on the screen, for example, in menus or dialog boxes, appear in the text like this: "Clicking the **Next** button moves you to the next screen."

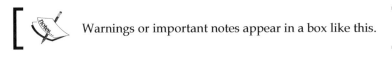

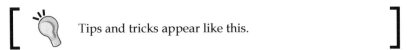

[viii]

Reader feedback

Feedback from our readers is always welcome. Let us know what you think about this book—what you liked or disliked. Reader feedback is important for us as it helps us develop titles that you will really get the most out of.

To send us general feedback, simply e-mail `feedback@packtpub.com`, and mention the book's title in the subject of your message.

If there is a topic that you have expertise in and you are interested in either writing or contributing to a book, see our author guide at `www.packtpub.com/authors`.

Customer support

Now that you are the proud owner of a Packt book, we have a number of things to help you to get the most from your purchase.

Downloading the example code

You can download the example code files from your account at `http://www.packtpub.com` for all the Packt Publishing books you have purchased. If you purchased this book elsewhere, you can visit `http://www.packtpub.com/support` and register to have the files e-mailed directly to you.

Errata

Although we have taken every care to ensure the accuracy of our content, mistakes do happen. If you find a mistake in one of our books—maybe a mistake in the text or the code—we would be grateful if you could report this to us. By doing so, you can save other readers from frustration and help us improve subsequent versions of this book. If you find any errata, please report them by visiting `http://www.packtpub.com/submit-errata`, selecting your book, clicking on the **Errata Submission Form** link, and entering the details of your errata. Once your errata are verified, your submission will be accepted and the errata will be uploaded to our website or added to any list of existing errata under the Errata section of that title.

To view the previously submitted errata, go to `https://www.packtpub.com/books/content/support` and enter the name of the book in the search field. The required information will appear under the **Errata** section.

Piracy

Piracy of copyrighted material on the Internet is an ongoing problem across all media. At Packt, we take the protection of our copyright and licenses very seriously. If you come across any illegal copies of our works in any form on the Internet, please provide us with the location address or website name immediately so that we can pursue a remedy.

Please contact us at copyright@packtpub.com with a link to the suspected pirated material.

We appreciate your help in protecting our authors and our ability to bring you valuable content.

Questions

If you have a problem with any aspect of this book, you can contact us at questions@packtpub.com, and we will do our best to address the problem.

1
New Missions – New Tools

The espionage job is to gather and analyze data. This requires us to use computers and software tools.

However, a secret agent's job is not limited to collecting data. It involves processing, filtering, and summarizing data, and also involves confirming the data and assuring that it contains meaningful and actionable information.

Any aspiring agent would do well to study the history of the World War II English secret agent, code-named Garbo. This is an inspiring and informative story of how secret agents operated in war time.

We're going to look at a variety of complex missions, all of which will involve Python 3 to collect, analyze, summarize, and present data. Due to our previous successes, we've been asked to expand our role in a number of ways.

HQ's briefings are going to help agents make some technology upgrades. We're going to locate and download new tools for new missions that we're going to be tackling. While we're always told that a good agent doesn't speculate, the most likely reason for new tools is a new kind of mission and dealing with new kinds of data or new sources. The details will be provided in the official briefings.

Field agents are going to be encouraged to branch out into new modes of data acquisition. Internet of Things leads to a number of interesting sources of data. HQ has identified some sources that will push the field agents in new directions. We'll be asked to push the edge of the envelope.

We'll look at the following topics:

- Tool upgrades, in general. Then, we'll upgrade Python to the latest stable version. We'll also upgrade the **pip** utility so that we can download more tools.
- Reviewing the Python language. This will only be a quick summary.

[1]

- Our first real mission will be an upgrade to the Beautiful Soup package. This will help us in gathering information from HTML pages.
- After upgrading Beautiful Soup, we'll use this package to gather live data from a web site.
- We'll do a sequence of installations in order to prepare our toolkit for later missions.
- In order to build our own gadgets, we'll have to install the Arduino IDE.

This will give us the tools for a number of data gathering and analytical missions.

Background briefing on tools

The organization responsible for tools and technology is affectionately known as The Puzzle Palace. They have provided some suggestions on what we'll need for the missions that we've been assigned. We'll start with an overview of the state of art in Python tools that are handed down from one of the puzzle solvers.

Some agents have already upgraded to Python 3.4. However, not all agents have done this. It's imperative that we use the latest and greatest tools.

There are four good reasons for this, as follows:

- **Features**: Python 3.4 adds a number of additional library features that we can use. The list of features is available at `https://docs.python.org/3/whatsnew/3.4.html`.
- **Performance**: Each new version is generally a bit faster than the previous version of Python.
- **Security**: While Python doesn't have any large security holes, there are new security changes in Python.
- **Housecleaning**: There are a number of rarely used features that were and have been removed.

Some agents may want to start looking at Python 3.5. This release is anticipated to include some optional features to provide data type hints. We'll look at this in a few specific cases as we go forward with the mission briefings. The type-analysis features can lead to improvements in the quality of the Python programming that an agent creates. The puzzle palace report is based on intelligence gathered at PyCon 2015 in Montreal, Canada. Agents are advised to follow the **Python Enhancement Proposals (PEP)** closely. Refer to `https://www.python.org/dev/peps/`.

Chapter 1

We'll focus on Python 3.4. For any agent who hasn't upgraded to Python 3.4.3, we'll look at the best way to approach this.

If you're comfortable with working on your own, you can try to move further and download and install Python 3.5. Here, the warning is that it's very new and it may not be quite as robust as the Python version 3.4. Refer to PEP 478 (`https://www.python.org/dev/peps/pep-0478/`) for more information about this release.

Doing a Python upgrade

It's important to consider each major release of Python as an add-on and not a replacement. Any release of Python 2 should be left in place. Most field agents will have several side-by-side versions of Python on their computers. The following are the two common scenarios:

- The OS uses Python 2. Mac OS X and Linux computers require Python 2; this is the default version of Python that's found when we enter `python` at the command prompt. We have to leave this in place.

- We might also have an older Python 3, which we used for the previous missions. We don't want to remove this until we're sure that we've got everything in place in order to work with Python 3.4.

We have to distinguish between the major, minor, and micro versions of Python. Python 3.4.3 and 3.4.2 have the same minor version (3.4). We can replace the micro version 3.4.2 with 3.4.3 without a second thought; they're always compatible with each other. However, we don't treat the minor versions quite so casually. We often want to leave 3.3 in place.

Generally, we do a field upgrade as shown in the following:

1. Download the installer that is appropriate for the OS and Python version. Start at this URL: `https://www.python.org/downloads/`. The web server can usually identify your computer's OS and suggest the appropriate download with a big, friendly, yellow button. Mac OS X agents will notice that we now get a `.pkg` (**package**) file instead of a `.dmg` (**disk image**) containing `.pkg`. This is a nice simplification.

2. When installing a new minor version, make sure to install in a new directory: keep 3.3 separate from 3.4. When installing a new micro version, replace any existing installation; replace 3.4.2 with 3.4.3.

   ◦ For Mac OS X and Linux, the installers will generally use names that include `python3.4` so that the minor versions are kept separate and the micro versions replace each other.

[3]

New Missions – New Tools

- ° For Windows, we have to make sure we use a distinct directory name based on the minor version number. For example, we want to install all new 3.4.*x* micro versions in `C:\Python34`. If we want to experiment with the Python 3.5 minor version, it would go in `C:\Python35`.

3. Tweak the `PATH` environment setting to choose the default Python.

   - ° This information is generally in our `~/.bash_profile` file. In many cases, the Python installer will update this file in order to assure that the newest Python is at the beginning of the string of directories that are listed in the `PATH` setting. This file is generally used when we log in for the first time. We can either log out and log back in again, or restart the terminal tool, or we can use the `source ~/.bash_profile` command to force the shell to refresh its environment.

   - ° For Windows, we must update the advanced system settings to tweak the value of the `PATH` environment variable. In some cases, this value has a huge list of paths; we'll need to copy the string and paste it in a text editor to make the change. We can then copy it from the text editor and paste it back in the environment variable setting.

4. After upgrading Python, use pip3.4 (or easy_install-3.4) to add the additional packages that we need. We'll look at some specific packages in mission briefings. We'll start by adding any packages that we use frequently.

At this point, we should be able to confirm that our basic toolset works. Linux and Mac OS agents can use the following command:

```
MacBookPro-SLott:Code slott$ python3.4
```

This should confirm that we've downloaded and installed Python and made it a part of our OS settings. The greeting will show which micro version of Python 3.4 have we installed.

For Windows, the command's name is usually just `python`. It would look similar to the following:

```
C:\> python
```

The Mac OS X interaction should include the version; it will look similar to the following code:

```
MacBookPro-SLott:NavTools-1.2 slott$ python3.4
Python 3.4.3 (v3.4.3:9b73f1c3e601, Feb 23 2015, 02:52:03)
[GCC 4.2.1 (Apple Inc. build 5666) (dot 3)] on darwin
```

Chapter 1

```
Type "help", "copyright", "credits" or "license" for more information.
>>> import sys
>>> sys.version_info
sys.version_info(major=3, minor=4, micro=3, releaselevel='final',
serial=0)
```

We've entered the **python3.4** command. This shows us that things are working very nicely. We have Python 3.4.3 successfully installed.

We don't want to make a habit of using the `python` or `python3` commands in order to run Python from the command line. These names are too generic and we could accidentally use Python 3.3 or Python 3.5, depending on what we have installed. We need to be intentional about using Python3.4.

Preliminary mission to upgrade pip

The first time that we try to use pip3.4, we may see an interaction as shown in the following:

```
MacBookPro-SLott:Code slott$ pip3.4 install anything
You are using pip version 6.0.8, however version 7.0.3 is available.
You should consider upgrading via the 'pip install --upgrade pip'
command.
```

The version numbers may be slightly different; this is not too surprising. The packaged version of **pip** isn't always the latest and greatest version. Once we've installed the Python package, we can upgrade **pip3.4** to the recent release. We'll use **pip** to upgrade itself.

It looks similar to the following code:

```
MacBookPro-SLott:Code slott$ pip3.4 install --upgrade pip
You are using pip version 6.0.8, however version 7.0.3 is available.
You should consider upgrading via the 'pip install --upgrade pip'
command.
Collecting pip from https://pypi.python.org/packages/py2.py3/p/pip/
pip-7.0.3-py2.py3-none-any.whl#md5=6950e1d775fea7ea50af690f72589dbd
  Downloading pip-7.0.3-py2.py3-none-any.whl (1.1MB)
    100% |###############################| 1.1MB 398kB/s
Installing collected packages: pip
  Found existing installation: pip 6.0.8
    Uninstalling pip-6.0.8:
      Successfully uninstalled pip-6.0.8

Successfully installed pip-7.0.3
```

[5]

New Missions – New Tools

We've run the pip installer to upgrade pip. We're shown some details about the files that are downloaded and new is version installed. We were able to do this with a simple `pip3.4` under Mac OS X.

Some packages will require system privileges that are available via the **sudo** command. While it's true that a few packages don't require system privileges, it's easy to assume that privileges are always required. For Windows, of course, we don't use **sudo** at all.

On Mac OS X, we'll often need to use `sudo -H` instead of simply using `sudo`. This option will make sure that the proper HOME environment variable is used to manage a cache directory.

Note that your actual results may differ from this example, depending on how out-of-date your copy of **pip** turns out to be. This `pip install --upgrade pip` is a pretty frequent operation as the features advance.

Background briefing: review of the Python language

Before moving on to our first mission, we'll review some essentials of the Python language, and the ways in which we'll use it to gather and disseminate data. We'll start by reviewing the interactive use of Python to do some data manipulation. Then we'll look at statements and script files.

When we start Python from the Terminal tool or the command line, we'll see an interaction that starts as shown in the following:

```
MacBookPro-SLott:Code slott$ python3.4
Python 3.4.3 (v3.4.3:9b73f1c3e601, Feb 23 2015, 02:52:03)
[GCC 4.2.1 (Apple Inc. build 5666) (dot 3)] on darwin
Type "help", "copyright", "credits" or "license" for more information.
>>>
```

The `>>>` prompt is Python's read-eval-print loop (REPL) that is waiting for us to enter a statement. If we use Python's development environment, IDLE, we'll also see this `>>>` prompt.

One of the simplest kinds of statements is a single expression. We can, for example, enter an arithmetic expression. The **Read Eval Print Loop (REPL)** will print the result automatically. Here's an example of simple math:

```
>>> 355/113
3.1415929203539825
```

We entered an expression statement and Python printed the resulting object. This gives us a way to explore the language. We can enter things and see the results, allowing us to experiment with new concepts.

Python offers us a number of different types of objects to work with. The first example showed integer objects, `355` and `113`, as well as a floating-point result object, `3.1415929203539825`.

In addition to integers and floats, we also have exact complex numbers. With the standard library, we can introduce decimal and fraction values using the `decimal` or `fractions` modules. Python can coerce values between the various types. If we have mixed values on either side of an operator, one of the values will be pushed up the numeric tower so that both operands have the same type. This means that integers can be promoted up to float and float can be promoted up to complex if necessary.

Python gives us a variety of operators. The common arithmetic operators are `+`, `-`, `*`, `/`, `//`, `%`, and `**`. These implement addition, subtraction, multiplication, true division, floor division, modulus, and raising to a power. The true division, `/`, will coerce integers to floating-point so that the answer is exact. The floor division, `//`, provides rounded-down answers, even with floating-point operands.

We also have some bit-fiddling operators: `~`, `&`, `|`, `^`, `<<`, and `>>`. These implement unary bitwise inversion, and, or, exclusive or, shift left, and shift right. These work with individual bits in a number. They're not logical operators at all.

What about more advanced math? We'll need to import libraries if we need more sophisticated features. For example, if we need to compute a square root, we'll need to import the `math` module, as follows:

```
>>> import math
>>> p= math.sqrt(7+math.sqrt(6+math.sqrt(5)))
```

Importing the `math` module creates a new object, `math`. This object is a kind of namespace that contains useful functions and constants. We'll use this `import` technique frequently to add features that we need to create useful software.

Using variables to save results

We can put a label on an object using the assignment statement. We often describe this as assigning an object to a variable; however, it's more like assigning a symbolic label to an object. The variable name (or label) must follow a specific set of syntax rules. It has to begin with a letter and can include any combination of letters, digits, and `_` characters. We'll often use simple words such as x, n, `samples`, and `data`. We can use `longer_names` where this adds clarity.

New Missions – New Tools

Using variables allows us to build up results in steps by assigning names to intermediate results. Here's an example:

```
>>> n = 355
>>> d = 113
>>> r = n/d
>>> result = "ratio: {0:.6f}".format(r)
>>> result
'ratio: 3.141593'
```

We assigned the n name to the 355 integer; then we assigned the d name to the 113 integer. Then we assigned the ratio to another variable, r.

We used the format() method for strings to create a new string that we assigned to the variable named result. The format() method starts with a format specification and replace {} with formatted versions of the argument values. In the {}'s object, we requested item 0 from the collection of arguments. Since Python's indexes always start from zero, this will be the first argument value. We used a format specification of .6f to show a floating-point value (f) with six digits to the right of the decimal point (.6). This formatted number was interpolated into the overall string and the resulting string was given the name result.

The last expression in the sequence of statements, result, is very simple. The result of this trivial expression is the value of the variable. It's a string that the REPL prints for us. We can use a similar technique to print the values of intermediate results such as the r variable. We'll often make heavy use of intermediate variables in order to expose the details of a calculation.

Using the sequence collections: strings

Python strings are a sequence of Unicode characters. We have a variety of quoting rules for strings. Here are two examples:

```
>>> 'String with " inside'
'String with " inside'
>>> "String's methods"
"String's methods"
```

We can either use quotes or apostrophes to delimit a string. In the likely event that a string contains both quotes and apostrophes, we can use a \' or \" to embed some punctuation; this is called an escape sequence. The initial \ escapes from the normal meaning of the next character. The following is an example showing the complicated quotes and escapes:

```
>>> "I said, \"Don't touch.\""
'I said, "Don\'t touch."'
```

[8]

Chapter 1

We used one set of quotes to enter the string. We used the escaped quotes in the string. Python responded with its preferred syntax; the canonical form for a string will generally use apostrophes to delimit the string overall.

Another kind of string that we'll encounter frequently is a byte string. Unlike a normal string that uses all the available Unicode characters, a byte string is limited to single-byte values. These can be shown using hexadecimal numeric codes, or – for 96 of the available bytes values – an ASCII character instead of a numeric value.

Here are two examples of byte strings:

```
>>> b'\x08\x09\x0a\x0c\x0d\x0e\x0f'
b'\x08\t\n\x0c\r\x0e\x0f'
>>> b'\x41\x53\x43\x49\x49'
b'ASCII'
```

In the first example, we provided hexadecimal values using the \xnn syntax for each byte. The prefix of \x means that the following values will be in base 16. We write base 16 values using the digits 0-9 along with the letters a-f. We provide seven values for \x08 to \x0f. Python replies using a canonical notation; our input follows more relaxed rules than those of Python's output. The canonical syntax is different for three important byte values: the tab character, \x08 can also be entered as \t. The newline character is most commonly entered as \n rather than \x0a. Finally, the carriage return character, \r, is shorter than \x0d.

In the second example, we also provided some hexadecimal values that overlap with some of the ASCII characters. Python's canonical form shows the ASCII characters instead of the hexadecimal values. This demonstrates that, for some byte values, ASCII characters are a handy shorthand.

In some applications, we'll have trouble telling a Unicode string, 'hello', from a byte string, b'hello'. We can add a u'hello' prefix in order to clearly state that this is a string of Unicode characters and not a string of bytes.

As a string is a collection of individual Unicode characters, we can extract the characters from a string using the character's index positions. Here's a number of examples:

```
>>> word = 'retackling'
>>> word[0]
'r'
>>> word[-1]
'g'
>>> word[2:6]
'tack'
>>> word[-3:]
'ing'
```

[9]

New Missions – New Tools

We've created a string, which is a sequence object. Sequence objects have items that can be addressed by their position or index. In position 0, we see the first item in the sequence, the 'r' character.

Sequences can also be indexed from the right to left using negative numbers. Position -1 is the last (rightmost) item in a sequence. Index position -2 is next-to-rightmost.

We can also extract a slice from a sequence. This is a new sequence that is copied from the original sequence. When we take items in positions 2 to 6, we get four characters with index values 2, 3, 4, and 5. Note that a slice includes the first position and never includes the last specified position, it's an upto but not including rule. Mathematicians call it a half-open interval and write it as [2, 6) or sometimes [2, 6[. We can use the following set comprehension rule to understand how the interval works:

$$\{x \mid 2 \le x < 6\}$$

All of the sequence collections allow us to count occurrences of an item and location the index of an item. The following are some examples that show the method syntax and the two universal methods that apply to sequences:

```
>>> word.count('a')
1
>>> word.index('t')
2
>>> word.index('z')
Traceback (most recent call last):
  File "<stdin>", line 1, in <module>
ValueError: substring not found
```

We've counted the number of items that match a particular value. We've also asked for the position of a given letter. This returns a numeric value for the index of the item equal to 't'.

String sequences have dozens of other methods to create new strings in various ways. We can do a large number of sophisticated manipulations.

Note that a string is an immutable object. We can't replace a character in a string. We can only build new strings from the old strings.

Chapter 1

Using other common sequences: tuples and lists

We can create two other common kinds of sequences: the list and the tuple. A tuple is a fixed-length sequence of items. We often use tuples for simple structures such as pairs (latitude, longitude) or triples (r, g, b). We write a literal tuple by enclosing the items in `()`s. It looks as shown in the following:

```
>>> ultramarine_blue = (63, 38, 191)
```

We've create a three-tuple or triple with some RGB values that comprise a color.

Python's assignment statement can tease a tuple into its individual items. Here's an example:

```
>>> red, green, blue = ultramarine_blue
>>> red
63
>>> blue
191
```

This multiple-variable assignment works well with tuples as a tuple has a fixed size. We can also address individual items of a tuple with expressions such as `ultramarine_blue[0]`. Slicing a tuple is perfectly legal; however, semantically a little murky. Why is `ultramarine_blue[:2]` used to create a pair from the red and green channel?

A list is a variable-length sequence of items. This is a mutable object and we can insert, append, remove, and replace items in the list. This is one of the profound differences between the tuple and list sequences. A tuple is immutable; once we've built it, we can't change it. A list is mutable.

The following is an example of a list that we can tweak in order to correct the errors in the data:

```
>>> samples = [8.04, 6.95, 0, 8.81, 8.33, 9.96, 7.24, 4.26, 10.84,
4.82]
>>> samples[2]= 7.58
>>> samples.append(5.68)
>>> samples
[8.04, 6.95, 7.58, 8.81, 8.33, 9.96, 7.24, 4.26, 10.84, 4.82, 5.68]
>>> sum(samples)
82.51000000000002
>>> round(sum(samples)/len(samples),2)
7.5
```

[11]

We've created a list object, samples, and initialized it with 10 values. We've set the value with an index of two; replacing a the zero item with 7.58. We've appended an item at the end of the list.

We've also shown two handy functions that apply to all sequences. However, they're particularly useful for lists. The `sum()` function adds up the values, reducing the list to a single value. The `len()` function counts the items, also reducing the list to a single value.

Note the awkward value shown for the sum; this is an important feature of floating-point numbers. In order to be really fast, they're finite. As they have a limited number of bits, they're only an approximation. Therefore, sometimes, we'll see some consequences of working with approximations.

> Floating-point numbers aren't mathematical abstractions. They're finite approximations. Sometimes, you'll see tiny error values.

One other interesting operator for sequences is the `in` comparison:

```
>>> 7.24 in samples
True
```

This checks whether a given item is found somewhere in the sequence. If we want the index of a given item, we can use the index method:

```
samples.index(7.24)
```

Using the dictionary mapping

The general idea of mapping is the association between keys and values. We might have a key of `'ultramarine blue'` associated with a value of the tuple, `(63, 38, 191)`. We might have a key of `'sunset orange'` associated with a tuple of `(254, 76, 64)`. We can represent this mapping of string-to-tuple with a Python dictionary object, as follows:

```
>>> colors = {'ultramarine blue': (63, 38, 191), 'sunset orange':
(254, 76, 64) }
```

We've replaced the words associated with `:` and wrapped the whole in `{ }`s in order to create a proper dictionary. This is a mapping from color strings to RGB tuples.

Chapter 1

A dictionary is mutable; we can add new key-value pairs and remove key-value mappings from it. Of course, we can interrogate a dictionary to see what keys are present and what value is associated with a key.

```
>>> colors['olive green'] = (181, 179, 92)
>>> colors.pop('sunset orange')
(254, 76, 64)
>>> colors['ultramarine blue']
(63, 38, 191)
>>> 'asparagus' in colors
False
```

The same syntax will replace an existing key in a dictionary with a new value. We can pop a key from the dictionary; this will both update the dictionary to remove the key value pair and return the value associated with the key. When we use syntax such as `colors['ultramarine blue']`, we'll retrieve the value associated with a given key.

The `in` operator checks to see whether the given item is one of the keys of the mapping. In our example, we didn't provide a mapping for the name `'asparagus'`.

We can retrieve the keys, the values, and the key value pairs from a mapping with methods of the class:

```
>>> sorted(colors.items())
[('olive green', (181, 179, 92)), ('ultramarine blue', (63, 38, 191))]
```

The `keys()` method returns the keys in the mapping. The `values()` method returns a list of only the values. The `items()` method returns a list of two-tuples. Each tuple is a key, value pair. We've applied the `sorted()` function in this example, as a dictionary doesn't guarantee any particular order for the keys. In many cases, we don't particularly care about the order. In the cases where we need to enforce the order, this is a common technique.

Comparing data and using the logic operators

Python implements a number of comparisons. We have the usual `==`, `!=`, `<=`, `>=`, `<`, and `>` operators. These provide the essential comparison capabilities. The result of a comparison is a boolean object, either `True` or `False`.

The boolean objects have their own special logic operators: `and`, `or`, and `not`. These operators can short-circuit the expression evaluation. In the case of `and`, if the left-hand side expression is `False`, the final result must be `False`; therefore, the right-hand side expression is not evaluated. In the case of `or`, the rules are reversed. If the left-hand side expression is `True`, the final result is already known to be `True`, so the right-hand side expression is skipped.

New Missions – New Tools

For example, take two variables, sum and count, as follows:

```
>>> sum
82.51
>>> count
11
>>> mean = count != 0 and sum/count
```

Let's look closely at the final expression. The left-hand side expression of the and operator is count != 0, which is True. Therefore, the right-hand side expression must be evaluated. Interestingly, the right-hand side object is the final result. A numeric value of 7.5 is the value of the mean variable.

The following is another example to show how the and operator behaves:

```
>>> sum
0.0
>>> count
0
>>> mean = count != 0 and sum/count
```

What happens here? The left-hand side expression of the and operator is count != 0, which is False. The right-hand side is not evaluated. There's no division by zero error exception raised by this. The final result is False.

Using some simple statements

All of the preceding examples focused on one-line expression statements. We entered an expression in REPL, Python evaluated the expression, and REPL helpfully printed the resulting value. While the expression statement is handy for experiments at the REPL prompt, there's one expression statement that agents use a lot, as shown in the following:

```
>>> print("Hello \N{EARTH}")
Hello ♁
```

The print() function prints the results on the console. We provided a string with a Unicode character that's not directly available on most keyboards, this is the **EARTH** character, ♁, U+2641, which looks different in different fonts.

We'll need the print() function as soon as we stop using interactive Python. Our scripts won't show any results unless we print them.

The other side of printing is the input() function. This will present a prompt and then read a string of input that is typed by a user at the console. We'll leave it to the interested agent to explore the details of how this works.

Chapter 1

We'll need more kinds of imperative statements to get any real work done. We've shown two forms of the assignment statement; both will put a label on an object. The following are two examples to put label on an object:

```
>>> n, d = 355, 113
>>> pi = n/d
```

The first assignment statement evaluated the 355, 115 expression and created a tuple object from two integer objects. In some contexts, the surrounding () s for a tuple are optional; this is one of those contexts. Then, we used multiple assignments to decompose the tuple to its two items and put labels on each object.

The second assignment statement follows the same pattern. The n/d expression is evaluated. It uses true division to create a floating-point result from integer operands. The resulting object has the name pi applied to it by the assignment statement.

Using compound statements for conditions: if

For conditional processing, we use the if statement. Python allows an unlimited number of else-if (elif) clauses, allowing us to build rather complex logic very easily.

For example, here's a statement that determines whether a value, n, is divisible by three, or five, or both:

```
>>> if n % 3 == 0 and n % 5 == 0:
...     print("fizz-buzz")
... elif n % 3 == 0:
...     print("fizz")
... elif n % 5 == 0:
...     print("buzz")
... else:
...     print(n)
```

We've written three Boolean expressions. The if statement will evaluate these in top-to-bottom order. If the value of the n variable is divisible by both, three and five, the first condition is True and the indented suite of statements is executed. In this example, the indented suite of statements is a single expression statement that uses the print() function.

If the first expression is False, then the elif clauses are examined in order. If none of the elif clauses are true, the indented suite of statements in the else clause is executed.

[15]

Remember that the and operator has a short-circuit capability. The first expression may involve as little as evaluating n % 3 == 0. If this subexpression is False, the entire and expression must be False; this means that the entire if clause is not executed. Otherwise, the entire expression must be evaluated.

Notice that Python changes the prompt from >>> at the start of a compound statement to ... to show that more of the statement can be entered. This is a helpful hint. We indent each suite of statements in a clause. We enter a blank line in order to show we're at the very end of the compound statement.

> This longer statement shows us an important syntax rule:
> Compound statements rely on indentation. Indent consistently. Use four spaces.

The individual if and elif clauses are separated based on their indentation level. The keywords such as if, elif, and else are not indented. The suite of statements in each clause is indented consistently.

Using compound statements for repetition: for and while

When we want to process all the items in a list or the lines in a file, we're going to use the for statement. The for statement allows us to specify a target variable, a source collection of values, and a suite of statements. The idea is that each item from the source collection is assigned to the target value and the suite of statements is executed.

The following is a complete example that computes the variance of some measurements:

```
>>> samples = [8.04, 6.95, 7.58, 8.81, 8.33, 9.96, 7.24, 4.26, 10.84, 4.82, 5.68]
>>> sum, sum2 = 0, 0
>>> for x in samples:
...     sum += x
...     sum2 += x**2
>>> n = len(samples)
>>> var = (sum2-(sum**2/n))/(n-1)
```

We've started with a list of values, assigned to the samples variable, plus two other variables, sum and sum2, to which we've assigned initial values of 0.

The `for` statement will iterate through the item in the `samples` list. An item will be assigned to the target variable, `x`, and then the indented body of the for statement is executed. We've written two assignment statements that will compute the new values for `sum` and `sum2`. These use the augmented assignment statement; using `+=` saves us from writing `sum = sum + x`.

After the `for` statement, we are assured that the body has been executed for all values in the source object, `samples`. We can save the count of the samples in a handy local variable, `n`. This makes the calculation of the variance slightly more clear. In this example, the variance is about 4.13.

The result is a number that shows how spread out the raw data is. The square root of the variance is the standard deviation. We expect two-third of our data points to lie in one standard deviation of the average. We often use variance when comparing two data sets. When we get additional data, perhaps from a different agent, we can compare the averages and variances to see whether the data is similar. If the variances aren't the same, this may reflect that there are different sources and possibly indicate that we shouldn't trust either of the agents that are supplying us this raw data. If the variances are identical, we have another question whether we being fed false information?

The most common use of the `for` statement is to visit each item in a collection. A slightly less common use is to iterate a finite number of times. We use a `range()` object to emit a simple sequence of integer values, as follows:

```
>>> list(range(5))
[0, 1, 2, 3, 4]
```

This means that we can use a statement such as `for i in range(n):` in order to iterate n times.

Defining functions

It's often important to decompose large, complex data acquisition and analysis problems into smaller, more solvable problems. Python gives us a variety of ways to organize our software. We have a tall hierarchy that includes packages, modules, classes, and functions. We'll start with function definitions as a way to decompose and reuse functionality. The later missions will require class definitions.

A function—mathematically—is a mapping from objects in a domain to objects in a range. Many mathematical examples map numbers to different numbers. For example, the arctangent function, available as `math.atan()`, maps a tangent value to the angle that has this tangent value. In many cases, we'll need to use `math.atan2()`, as our tangent value is a ratio of the lengths of two sides of a triangle; this function maps a pair of values to a single result.

New Missions – New Tools

In Python terms, a function has a name and a collection of parameters and it may return a distinct value. If we don't explicitly return a resulting value, a function maps its values to a special None object.

Here's a handy function to average the values in a sequence:

```
>>> def mean(data):
...     if len(data) == 0:
...         return None
...     return sum(data)/len(data)
```

This function expects a single parameter, a sequence of values to average. When we evaluate the function, the argument value will be assigned to the data parameter. If the sequence is empty, we'll return the special None object in order to indicate that there's no average when there's no data.

If the sequence isn't empty, we'll divide the sum by the count to compute the average. Since we're using exact division, this will return a floating-point value even if the sequence is all integers.

The following is how it looks when we use our newly minted function combined with built-in functions:

```
>>> samples = [8.04, 6.95, 7.58, 8.81, 8.33, 9.96, 7.24, 4.26, 10.84,
4.82, 5.68]
>>> round(mean(samples), 2)
7.5
```

We've computed the mean of the values in the samples variable using our mean() function. We've applied the round() function to the resulting value to show that the mean is rounded to two decimal places.

Creating script files

We shouldn't try to do all the our data gathering and analysis by entering the Python code interactively at the >>> prompt. It's possible to work this way; however, the copy and paste is tedious and error-prone. It's much better to create a Python script that will gather, analyze, and display useful intelligence assets that we've gathered (or purchased).

A Python script is a file of Python statements. While it's not required, it's helpful to be sure that the file's name is a valid Python symbol that is created with letters, numbers, and _'s. It's also helpful if the file's name ends with .py.

Here's a simple script file that shows some of the features that we've been looking at:

```python
import random, math
samples = int(input("How many samples: "))
inside = 0
for i in range(samples):
    if math.hypot(random.random(), random.random()) <= 1.0:
        inside += 1
print(inside, samples, inside/samples, math.pi/4)
```

This script file can be given a name such as `example1.py`. The script will use the `input()` function to prompt the user for a number of random samples. Since the result of `input()` is a string, we'll need to convert the string to an integer in order to be able to use it. We've initialized a variable, `inside`, to zero.

The `for` statement will execute the indented body for the number of times that are given by the value of samples. The `range()` object will generate `samples` distinct integer values. In the `for` statement, we've used an `if` statement to filter some randomly generated values. The values we're examining are the result of `math.hypot(random.random(), random.random())`. What is this value? It's the hypotenuse of a right angled triangle with sides that are selected randomly. We'll leave it to each field agent to rewrite this script in order to assign and print some intermediate variables to show precisely how this calculation works.

We're looking at a triangle with one vertex at $(0,0)$ and another at (x,y). The third vertex could either be at $(0,y)$ or $(x,0)$, the results don't depend on how we visualize the triangle. Since the triangle sides are selected randomly, the end point of the hypotenuse can be any value from $(0,0)$ to $(1,1)$; the length of this varies between 0 and $\sqrt{2}$.

Statistically, we expect that most of the points should lie in a circle with a radius of one. How many should lie in this quarter circle? Interestingly, the random distribution will have $\dfrac{\pi}{4}$ of the samples in the circle; $1-\dfrac{\pi}{4}$ will be outside the circle.

When working in counterintelligence, the data that we're providing needs to be plausible. If we're going to mislead, our fake data needs to fit the basic statistical rules. A careful study of history will show how *Operation Mincemeat* was used to deceive Axis powers during World War II. What's central to this story is the plausibility of every nuance of the data that is supplied.

New Missions – New Tools

Mission One – upgrade Beautiful Soup

It seems like the first practical piece of software that every agent needs is Beautiful Soup. We often make extensive use of this to extract meaningful information from HTML web pages. A great deal of the world's information is published in the HTML format. Sadly, browsers must tolerate broken HTML. Even worse, website designers have no incentive to make their HTML simple. This means that HTML extraction is something every agent needs to master.

Upgrading the Beautiful Soup package is a core mission that sets us up to do more useful espionage work. First, check the PyPI description of the package. Here's the URL: `https://pypi.python.org/pypi/beautifulsoup4`. The language is described as Python 3, which is usually a good indication that the package will work with any release of Python 3.

To confirm the Python 3 compatibility, track down the source of this at the following URL:

`http://www.crummy.com/software/BeautifulSoup/`.

This page simply lists Python 3 without any specific minor version number. That's encouraging. We can even look at the following link to see more details of the development of this package:

`https://groups.google.com/forum/#!forum/beautifulsoup`

The installation is generally just as follows:

`MacBookPro-SLott:Code slott$ sudo pip3.4 install beautifulsoup4`

Windows agents can omit the **sudo** prefix.

This will use the **pip** application to download and install BeautifulSoup. The output will look as shown in the following:

```
Collecting beautifulsoup4
  Downloading beautifulsoup4-4.3.2.tar.gz (143kB)
    100% |████████████████████████████████| 143kB 1.1MB/s
Installing collected packages: beautifulsoup4
  Running setup.py install for beautifulsoup4
Successfully installed beautifulsoup4-4.3.2
```

Note that Pip 7 on Macintosh uses the ▉ character instead of # to show status. The installation was reported as successful. That means we can start using the package to analyze the data.

We'll finish this mission by gathering and parsing a very simple page of data.

We need to help agents make the sometimes dangerous crossing of the Gulf Stream between Florida and the Bahamas. Often, Bimini is used as a stopover; however, some faster boats can go all the way from Florida to Nassau in a single day. On a slower boat, the weather can change and an accurate multi-day forecast is essential.

The Georef code for this area is GHLL140032. For more information, look at the 25°32'N 79°46'W position on a world map. This will show the particular stretch of ocean for which we need to supply forecast data.

Here's a handy URL that provides weather forecasts for agents who are trying to make the passage between Florida and the Bahamas:

http://forecast.weather.gov/shmrn.php?mz=amz117&syn=amz101.

This page includes a weather synopsis for the overall South Atlantic (the amz101 zone) and a day-by-day forecast specific to the Bahamas (the amz117 zone). We want to trim this down to the relevant text.

Getting an HTML page

The first step in using BeautifulSoup is to get the HTML page from the US National Weather Service and parse it in a proper document structure. We'll use urllib to get the document and create a Soup structure from that. Here's the essential processing:

```
from bs4 import BeautifulSoup
import urllib.request
query= "http://forecast.weather.gov/shmrn.php?mz=amz117&syn=amz101"
with urllib.request.urlopen(query) as amz117:
    document= BeautifulSoup(amz117.read())
```

We've opened a URL and assigned the file-like object to the amz117 variable. We've done this in a with statement. Using with will guarantee that all network resources are properly disconnected when the execution leaves the indented body of the statement.

In the with statement, we've read the entire document available at the given URL. We've provided the sequence of bytes to the BeautifulSoup parser, which creates a parsed Soup data structure that we can assign to the document variable.

The with statement makes an important guarantee; when the indented body is complete, the resource manager will close. In this example, the indented body is a single statement that reads the data from the URL and parses it to create a BeautifulSoup object. The resource manager is the connection to the Internet based on the given URL. We want to be absolutely sure that all operating system (and Python) resources that make this open connection work are properly released. This release when finished guarantees what the with statement offers.

New Missions – New Tools

Navigating the HTML structure

HTML documents are a mixture of tags and text. The parsed structure is iterable, allowing us to work through text and tags using the `for` statement. Additionally, the parsed structure contains numerous methods to search for arbitrary features in the document.

Here's the first example of using methods names to pick apart a document:

```
content= document.body.find('div', id='content').div
```

When we use a tag name, such as `body`, as an attribute name, this is a search request for the first occurrence of that tag in the given container. We've used `document.body` to find the `<body>` tag in the overall HTML document.

The `find()` method finds the first matching instance using more complex criteria than the tag's name. In this case, we've asked to find `<div id="content">` in the `body` tag of the document. In this identified `<div>`, we need to find the first nested `<div>` tag. This division has the synopsis and forecast.

The content in this division consists of a mixed sequence of text and tags. A little searching shows us that the synopsis text is the fifth item. Since Python sequences are based at zero, this has an index of four in the `<div>`. We'll use the `contents` attribute of a given object to identify tags or text blocks by position in a document object.

The following is how we can get the synopsis and forecast. Once we have the forecast, we'll need to create an iterator for each day in the forecast:

```
synopsis = content.contents[4]
forecast = content.contents[5]
strong_list = list(forecast.findAll('strong'))
timestamp_tag, *forecast_list = strong_list
```

We've extracted the synopsis as a block of text. HTML has a quirky feature of an `<hr>` tag that contains the forecast. This is, in principle, invalid HTML. Even though it seems invalid, browsers tolerate it. It has the data that we want, so we're forced to work with it as we find it.

In the forecast `<hr>` tag, we've used the `findAll()` method to create a list of the sequence of `<strong>` tags. These tags are interleaved between blocks of text. Generally, the text in the tag tells us the day and the text between the `<strong>` tags is the forecast for that day. We emphasize generally as there's a tiny, but important special case.

Chapter 1

Due to the special case, we've split the `strong_list` sequence into a head and a tail. The first item in the list is assigned to the `timestamp_tag` variable. All the remaining items are assigned to the `forecast_list` variable. We can use the value of `timestamp_tag.string` to recover the string value in the tag, which will be the timestamp for the forecast.

Your extension to this mission is to parse this with `datetime.datetime.strptime()`. It will improve the overall utility of the data in order to replace strings with proper `datetime` objects.

The value of the `forecast_list` variable is an alternating sequence of `<strong>` tags and forecast text. Here's how we can extract these pairs from the overall document:

```
for strong in forecast_list:
    desc= strong.string.strip()
    print( desc, strong.nextSibling.string.strip() )
```

We've written a loop to step through the rest of the `<strong>` tags in the `forecast_list` object. Each item is a highlighted label for a given day. The value of `strong.nextSibling` will be the document object after the `<strong>` tag. We can use `strong.nextSibling.string` to extract the string from this block of text; this will be the details of the forecast.

We've used the `strip()` method of the string to remove extraneous whitespace around the forecast elements. This makes the resulting text block more compact.

With a little more cleanup, we can have a tidy forecast that looks similar to the following:

```
TONIGHT 2015-06-30
-------------------
E TO SE WINDS 10 TO 15 KT...INCREASING TO 15 TO 20 KT
 LATE. SEAS 3 TO 5 FT ATLC EXPOSURES...AND 2 FT OR LESS
 ELSEWHERE.
WED 2015-07-01
-------------------
E TO SE WINDS 15 TO 20 KT...DIMINISHING TO 10 TO 15 KT
 LATE. SEAS 4 TO 6 FT ATLC EXPOSURES...AND 2 FT OR
 LESS ELSEWHERE.
```

>
> **Downloading the example code**
> You can download the example code files from your account at `http://www.packtpub.com` for all the Packt Publishing books you have purchased. If you purchased this book elsewhere, you can visit `http://www.packtpub.com/support` and register to have the files e-mailed directly to you.

New Missions – New Tools

We've stripped away a great deal of HTML overhead. We've reduced the forecast to the barest facts. With a little more fiddling, we can get it down to a pretty tiny block of text. We might want to represent this in **JavaScript Object Notation (JSON)**. We can then encrypt the JSON string before the transmission. Then, we could use steganography to embed the encrypted text in another kind of document in order to transmit to a friendly ship captain that is working the route between Key Biscayne and Bimini. It may look as if we're just sending each other pictures of rainbow butterfly unicorn kittens.

This mission demonstrates that we can use Python 3, `urllib`, and BeautifulSoup. Now, we've got a working environment.

Doing other upgrades

When we upgrade to Python 3.4, we often need to upgrade the packages that we had previously been working with in the older versions of Python. We find that we often need to remind the field agents that software upgrades may be boring and mundane work; however, every mission is built on a foundation of software in order to process the intelligence data.

It's important to be sure that we can process graphics and images. That means we'll need a copy of Pillow, a project that maintains the Python Imaging Library.

Here's how this upgrade will look:

```
MacBookPro-SLott:doc slott$ pip3.4 install pillow
Collecting pillow
  Downloading Pillow-2.9.0-cp34-cp34m-macosx_10_6_intel.macosx_10_9_
intel.macosx_10_9_x86_64.macosx_10_10_intel.macosx_10_10_x86_64.whl
(2.9MB)
    100% |████████████████████████████████| 2.9MB 178kB/s
Installing collected packages: pillow
Successfully installed pillow-2.9.0
```

This means that we can continue to process graphics successfully. For more information on Pillow, refer to *Python for Secret Agents* 1st Edition.

Also, refer to `https://python-pillow.github.io` and `http://pillow.readthedocs.org`.

We'll start using this package in *Chapter 3, Following the Social Network*.

[24]

Mission to expand our toolkit

Now that we know our Python 3 is up-to-date, we can add some additional tools. We'll be using several advanced packages to help in acquiring and analyzing raw data.

We're going to need to tap into the social network. There are a large number of candidate social networks that we could mine for information. We'll start with Twitter. We can access the Twitter feed using direct API requests. Rather than working through the protocols at a low level, we'll make use of a Python package that provides some simplifications.

Our first choice is the Twitter API project on PyPI, as follows: `https://pypi.python.org/pypi/TwitterAPI/2.3.3`.

This can be installed using `sudo pip3.4 install twitterapi`.

We have some alternatives, one of which is the Twitter project from sixohsix. Here's the URL: `https://pypi.python.org/pypi/twitter/1.17.0`.

We can install this using `sudo pip3.4 install twitter`.

We'll focus on the twitterapi package. Here's what happens when we do the installation:

```
MacBookPro-SLott:Code slott$ sudo -H pip3.4 install twitterapi
Password:
Collecting twitterapi
  Downloading TwitterAPI-2.3.3.1.tar.gz
Collecting requests (from twitterapi)
  Downloading requests-2.7.0-py2.py3-none-any.whl (470kB)
    100% |████████████████████████████████| 471kB 751kB/s
Collecting requests-oauthlib (from twitterapi)
  Downloading requests_oauthlib-0.5.0-py2.py3-none-any.whl
Collecting oauthlib>=0.6.2 (from requests-oauthlib->twitterapi)
  Downloading oauthlib-0.7.2.tar.gz (106kB)
    100% |████████████████████████████████| 106kB 1.6MB/s
Installing collected packages: requests, oauthlib, requests-oauthlib,
twitterapi
  Running setup.py install for oauthlib
  Running setup.py install for twitterapi
Successfully installed oauthlib-0.7.2 requests-2.7.0 requests-
oauthlib-0.5.0 twitterapi-2.3.3.1
```

New Missions – New Tools

We used the `sudo -H` option, as required by Mac OS X. Windows agents would omit this. Some Linux agents can omit the `-H` option as it may be the default behavior.

Note that four packages were installed. The `twitterapi` package included the `requests` and `requests-oauthlib` packages. This, in turn, required the `oauthlib` package, which was downloaded automatically for us.

The missions for using this package start in *Chapter 3, Following the Social Network*. For now, we'll count the installation as a successful preliminary mission.

Scraping data from PDF files

In addition to HTML, a great deal of data is packaged as PDF files. PDF files are designed as the requirements to produce the printed output consistently across a variety of devices. When we look at the structure of these documents, we find that we have a complex and compressed storage format. In this structure, there are fonts, rasterized images, and descriptions of text elements in a simplified version of the PostScript language.

There are several issues the come into play here, as follows:

- The files are quite complex. We don't want to tackle the algorithms that are required to read the streams encoded in the PDF since we're focused on the content.

- The content is organized for tidy printing. What we perceive as a single page of text is really just a collection of text blobs. We've been taught how to identify the text blobs as headers, footers, sidebars, titles, code examples, and other semantic features of a page. This is actually a pretty sophisticated bit of pattern matching. There's an implicit agreement between readers and book designers to stick to some rules to place the content on the pages.

- It's possible that a PDF can be created from a scanned image. This will require **Optical Character Recognition (OCR)** in order to recover useful text from the image.

In order to extract text from a PDF, we'll need to use a tool such as the PDF Miner 3k. Look for this package at `https://pypi.python.org/pypi/pdfminer3k/1.3.0`.

An alternative is the `pdf` package. You can look at:

`https://pypi.python.org/pypi/PDF/1.0` for the package.

In *Chapter 4, Dredging up History*, we'll look at the kinds of algorithms that we'll need to write in order to extract useful content from PDF files.

However, for now, we need to install this package in order to be sure that we can process PDF files. We'll use `sudo -H pip3.4 install pdfminer3k` to do the installation. The output looks as shown in the following:

```
MacBookPro-SLott:Code slott$ sudo -H pip3.4 install pdfminer3k
Collecting pdfminer3k
  Downloading pdfminer3k-1.3.0.tar.gz (9.7MB)
    100% |████████████████████████████████| 9.7MB 55kB/s
Collecting pytest>=2.0 (from pdfminer3k)
  Downloading pytest-2.7.2-py2.py3-none-any.whl (127kB)
    100% |████████████████████████████████| 131kB 385kB/s
Collecting ply>=3.4 (from pdfminer3k)
  Downloading ply-3.6.tar.gz (281kB)
    100% |████████████████████████████████| 282kB 326kB/s
Collecting py>=1.4.29 (from pytest>=2.0->pdfminer3k)
  Downloading py-1.4.30-py2.py3-none-any.whl (81kB)
    100% |████████████████████████████████| 86kB 143kB/s
Installing collected packages: py, pytest, ply, pdfminer3k
  Running setup.py install for ply
  Running setup.py install for pdfminer3k
Successfully installed pdfminer3k-1.3.0 ply-3.6 py-1.4.30 pytest-2.7.2
```

Windows agents will omit the `sudo -H` prefix. This is a large and complex installation. The package itself is pretty big (almost 10 Mb.) It requires additional packages such as `pytest`, and `py`. It also incorporates `ply`, which is an interesting tool in its own right.

Interestingly, the documentation for how to use this package can be hard to locate. Here's the link to locate it:

`http://www.unixuser.org/~euske/python/pdfminer/index.html`.

Note that the documentation is older than the actual package as it says (in red) Python 3 is not supported. However, the `pdfminer3k` project clearly states that `pdfminer3k` is a Python 3 port of `pdfminer`. While the software may have been upgraded, some of the documentation still needs work.

We can learn more about `ply` here at `https://pypi.python.org/pypi/ply/3.6`. The `lex` and `yacc` summary may not be too helpful for most of the agents. These terms refer to the two classic programs that are widely used to create the tools that support software development.

Sidebar on the ply package

When we work with the Python language, we rarely give much thought on how the **Python** program actually works. We're mostly interested in results, not the details of how Python language statements lead to useful processing by the Python program. The `ply` package solves the problem of translating characters to meaningful syntax.

Agents that are interested in the details of how Python works will need to consider the source text that we write. When we write the Python code, we're writing a sequence of intermingled keywords, symbols, operators, and punctuation. These various language elements are just sequences of Unicode characters that follow a strict set of rules. One wrong character and we get errors from Python.

There's a two-tier process to translate a `.py` file of the source text to something that is actionable.

At the lowest tier, an algorithm must do the lexical scanning of our text. A lexical scanner identifies the keywords, symbols, literals, operators, and punctuation marks; the generic term for these various language elements is tokens. A classic program to create lexical scanners is called `lex`. The `lex` program uses a set of rules to transform a sequence of characters into a sequence of higher-level tokens.

The process of compiling Python tokens to useful statements is the second tier. The classic program for this is called **Yacc (Yet Another Compiler Compiler)**. The yacc language contained the rules to interpret a sequence of tokens as a valid statement in the language. Associated with the rules to parse a target language, the yacc language also contained statements for an action to be taken when the statement was recognized. The yacc program compiles the rules and statements into a new program that we call a compiler.

The `ply` Python package implements both the tiers. We can use it to define a lexical scanner and a parser that is based on the the classic lex and yacc concepts. Software developers will use a tool such as `ply` to process statements in a well-defined formal language.

Building our own gadgets

Sometimes, we need to move beyond the data that is readily available on computers. We might need to build our own devices for espionage. There are a number of handy platforms that we can use to build our own sensors and gadgets. These are all single-board computers. These computers have a few high-level interfaces, often USB-based, along with a lot of low-level interfaces that allow us to create simple and interactive devices.

To work with these, we'll create a software on a large computer, such as a laptop or desktop system. We'll upload our software to our a single board computer and experiment with the gadget that we're building.

There are a variety of these single board computers. Two popular choices are the Raspberry Pi and the Arduino. One of the notable differences between these devices is that a Raspberry Pi runs a small GNU/Linux operating system, where as an Arduino doesn't offer much in the way of OS features.

Both devices allow us to create simple, interactive devices. There are ways to run Python on Raspberry Pi using the RPi GPIO module. Our gadget development needs to focus on Arduino as there is a rich variety of hardware that we can use. We can find small, robust Arduinos that are suitable for harsh environments.

A simple Arduino Uno isn't the only thing that we'll need. We'll also need some sensors and wires. We'll save the detailed shopping list for *Chapter 5, Data Collection Gadgets*. At this point, we're only interested in software tools.

Getting the Arduino IDE

To work with Arduino, we'll need to download the Arduino Integrated Development Environment (IDE.) This will allow us to write programs in the Arduino language, upload them to our Arduino, and do some basic debugging. An Arduino program is called a sketch.

We'll need to get the Arduino IDE from `https://www.arduino.cc/en/Main/ Software`. On the right-hand side of this web page, you can pick the OS for our working computer and download the proper Arduino tool set. Some agents prefer the idea of making a contribution to the Arduino foundation. However, it's possible to download the IDE without making a contribution.

For Mac OS X, the download will be a `.ZIP` file. This will unpack itself in the IDE application; we can copy this to our `Applications` folder and we're ready to go.

For Windows agents, we can download a `.MSI` file that will do the complete installation. This is preferred for computers where we have full administrative access. In some cases, where we may not have administrative rights, we'll need to download the `.ZIP` file, which we can unpack in a `C:\Arduino` directory.

We can open the Arduino application to see an initial sketch. The screen looks something similar to the following screenshot:

The sketch name will be based on the date on which you run the application. Also, the communications port shown in the lower right-hand corner may change, depending on whether your Arduino is plugged in.

Chapter 1

We don't want to do anything more than be sure that the Arduino IDE program runs. Once we see that things are working, we can quit the IDE application.

An alternative is the Fritzing application. Refer to `http://www.fritzing.org` for more information. We can use this software to create engineering diagrams and lists of parts for a particular gadget. In some cases, we can also use this to save software sketches that are associated with a gadget. The Arduino IDE is used by the Fritzing tool. Go to `http://fritzing.org/download/` to download Fritzing.

Getting a Python serial interface

In many cases, we'll want to have a more complex interaction between a desktop computer and an Arduino-based sensor. This will often lead to using the USB devices on our computer from our Python applications. If we want to interact directly with an Arduino (or other single-board computer) from Python, we'll need `PySerial`. An alternate is the **USPP (Universal Serial Port Python)** library. This allows us to communicate without having the Arduino IDE running on our computer. It allows us separate our data that is being gathered from our software development.

For PySerial, refer to `https://pypi.python.org/pypi/pyserial/2.7`. We can install this with `sudo -H pip3.4 install pyserial`.

Here's how the installation looks:

```
MacBookPro-SLott:Code slott$ sudo -H pip3.4 install pyserial
Password:
Collecting pyserial
  Downloading pyserial-2.7.tar.gz (122kB)
    100% |████████████████████████████████| 122kB 1.5MB/s
Installing collected packages: pyserial
  Running setup.py install for pyserial
Successfully installed pyserial-2.7
```

Windows agents will omit the **sudo -H** command. This command has downloaded and installed the small PySerial module.

We can leverage this to communicate with an Arduino (or any other device) through a USB port. We'll look at the interaction in *Chapter 5, Data Collection Gadgets*.

Summary

We've upgraded our toolkit in order to include the latest release of Python 3.4 (and even Python 3.5). We've upgraded Beautiful Soup, as well as added the Twitter API, PDFMiner 3K, and PySerial. This will give us the kind of tools that are required to gather and process a wide variety of information. We can even start building our own specialized gadgets based on the Arduino board.

In the next chapter, we'll start with some missions that will exploit our new Python 3.4 tools. We'll examine some foundational data gathering techniques. We'll look at how examining web server logs can reveal patterns of access. This is a kind of big data application since a busy web server can enjoy a lot of traffic.

Tracks, Trails, and Logs

In many cases, espionage is about data: primary facts and figures that help make an informed decision. It can be military, but it's more commonly economic or engineering in nature. Where's the best place to locate a new building? How well is the other team really doing? Among all of these prospects, which is the best choice?

In some cases, we're looking for data that's one step removed from the primary facts. We're might need to know who's downloading the current team statistics? Who's reading the press-release information? Who's writing the bulk of the comments in our comments section? Which documents are really being downloaded? What is the pattern of access?

We're going to get data about the users and sources of some primary data. It's commonly called metadata: data about the primary data. It's the lifeblood of counter-intelligence.

We'll get essential web server metadata first. We'll scrape our web server's logs for details of website traffic. One of the important questions we'll ask is who is making the requests? A web site that demands a login can use cookies to track viewers. A web site (or the introductory pages of a web site) where cookies aren't in use have to do a bit more work. We'll look at how we can track usage without cookies.

In this chapter, we'll cover the following topics:

- A background briefing on web servers and their logs
- How to write regular expressions for decomposing a web log into usable pieces of information
- Creating the tools needed to parse the Apache Common Log Format
- Using Python packages to read compressed files as well as download files from remote servers
- Analyzing logs to find out what users are downloading

[33]

Tracks, Trails, and Logs

- Using more advanced tools like the **Whois** program to see who's making the requests
- How to automate some of this extraction and analysis

This sequence of missions shows us how to reduce large volumes of raw data to summaries of useful information.

Background briefing – web servers and logs

At its heart, the World Wide Web is a vast collection of computers that handle the HTTP protocol. The HTTP protocol defines a request message and a response. A web server handles these requests, creating appropriate responses. This activity is written to a log, and we're interested in that log.

When we interact with a complex web site for a company that conducts e-business—buying or selling on the web—it can seem a lot more sophisticated than this simplistic request and reply protocol. This apparent complexity arises from an HTML web page, which includes JavaScript programming. This extra layer of code can make requests and process replies in ways that aren't obvious to the user of the site.

All web site processing begins with some initial request for an HTML web page. Other requests from JavaScript programs will be data requests that don't lead to a complete HTML page being sent from the server. It's common for JavaScript programs to request JSON data instead of an HTML page. **JSON** is short for **JavaScript Object Notation**, and it can summarize complex data in a relatively easy-to-use fashion.

A request for pure data is often called **Representational State Transfer (REST)**. A RESTful request describes a resource. The web server will create a representation of the state of that resource and transmit that representation. Often, this representation is in JSON notation. To the web server, a REST request in JSON and an HTML page request are the same thing: a request that leads to a response. They'll both show up in the log as requests.

Understanding the variety of formats

Web server logs have a format that's widely used: the Apache **Common Log Format (CLF)**. A server may adhere to the CLF, or the administrators may have made some local tweaks to expand or contract the amount of available data. Python gives an agent the flexibility to deal with logs files in their endless variety.

[34]

We'll focus on CLF as a starting point. By using Python's Regular Expression module, `re`, we'll be able to handle a number of variants with minimal programming changes.

Web server logs may also be compressed as ZIP files for download. We'll address automated unzipping and other physical format considerations as we go. We'll use the `zipfile` module to handle the overheads of dealing with zipped files. We'll try to create a kind of pipeline for processing that allows us to add or change processing elements.

Getting a web server log

An agent with a personal web site will have access to the sites logs. Many hosting services have options to save web logs for analysis. For example, the A2 hosting company offers a management console which allows the user to request that logs be saved for analysis. The user can then download the log. Or, more to the point, a Python script can download the log.

When using a service like Amazon's **Expandable Cloud Computing** (**EC2**), the agent will have to look a little more deeply into how Apache (or Tomcat or Nginx) logs work. While these servers are quite sophisticated, they often have configuration options for periodic log rotation that fits our need to see periodic details that we can summarize. See `http://httpd.apache.org/docs/2.4/logs.html` for more information on how this works.

In some cases, agents have a network of contacts that serve as a source for data like this. A few discrete questions placed in the right context can yield a great deal of assistance. Meetup groups for technology-minded people are a good place to locate more information. Maker fairs are also a helpful source of information. In some cases, contacts have reached out to experienced agents for help in analyzing logs.

Writing a regular expression for parsing

The logs look complex. Here's a sample line from a log:

```
109.128.44.217 - - [31/May/2015:22:55:59 -0400] "GET / HTTP/1.1"
200 14376 "-" "Mozilla/5.0 (iPad; CPU OS 8_1_2 like Mac OS X)
AppleWebKit/600.1.4 (KHTML, like Gecko) Version/8.0 Mobile/12B440
Safari/600.1.4"
```

How can we pick this apart? Python offers us regular expressions as a way to describe (and parse) this string of characters.

[**35**]

We write a regular expression as a way of defining a set of strings. The set can be very small and have only a single string in it, or the set can be large and describe an infinite number of related strings. We have two issues that we have to overcome: how do we specify infinite sets? How can we separate those characters that help specify a rule from characters that just mean themselves?

For example, we might write a regular expression like `aabr`. This specifies a set that contains a single string. This regular expression looks like the mathematical expression $a \times a \times b \times r$ that has been abbreviated by omitting explicit multiplication signs. Note that this implicit $\times$ operator isn't commutative like the integer $\times$. Mathematically, we could then abbreviate *aabr* as a^2br. Since the original ASCII character set lacked the necessary superscript numbers, we have to invent some more complex syntax to show the concept using only the available ASCII characters. Something like `a{2}br` is used for this. This is a good beginning, but it brings up two problems. What about indefinite repetition? What about matching { or } as characters?

How can we show an indefinite repetition of a character? While we could try to write a^xbr, that's not exactly what we mean. In some cases, we don't care about the value of x, the number of copies of a. Mathematically, we prefer to write a^*br to show that the first character in the string can be repeated any number of times, and we don't know or care how many times. Any number, in this case, can include zero copies of the first character. This means that the set of strings is $\{br, abr, aabr, aaabr, ...\}$.

Our keyboards don't quite have the typesetting flexibility that we need to be able to write regular expressions like this. We can't use the star as a superscript character: the * and □ characters can only sit in the middle of the line when working in a pure text file. This flat presentation can lead to some confusion when trying to read and write regular expressions.

To write regular expressions in a very general way, it would be nice to have some way to state rules, patterns, or classes of characters rather than merely individual characters to match. The problem is that any character we might want to use for writing rules or patterns is also a character we'd like to match!

Over the years, we've adopted the following conventions:

- Most characters—but not all—are **ordinary** characters and match themselves. For example, the regular expression a matches the character a.
- Some characters, specifically *, +, ?, |, ., [,], {, }, |, \,), and), are **special** characters because they're used to write rules or patterns. These characters don't simply match themselves.

[36]

- We'll use \ to escape the meaning of the following character. This will make an ordinary character special or a special character ordinary. For example, the regular expression * removes the special meaning of *, and now it matches *. The regular expression \d adds a special meaning to d, and now it matches any single decimal digit.

This leads us to regular expressions which will use a lot of \ characters. However, it's confusing that the Python language also uses \ escapes when writing a string literal. We have to distinguish between two contexts for string literals:

- **Ordinary Python Strings**: The default case is to have Python examine the string and replace escape sequences with otherwise unprintable characters. When we write '\u03c0\xd7r\xb2', we expect Python to replace the various escapes with proper Unicode characters; the escapes really mean this: 'π×r²'. Sometimes, we'll use the u' prefix for this: u'\u03c0\xd7r\xb2'.
- **Regular Expression Strings**: When writing regular expressions, we do not want Python messing with the \ characters. To do this, we'll use raw strings. We'll write regular expressions using r'.*\..*'. The alternative is to use \\ to stand for a single \ in the resulting string. We want to avoid '.*\\..*'.

Using raw strings for regular expressions will make our lives simpler.

Introducing some regular expression rules and patterns

One of the most useful features of regular expressions is using a symbol to match single character in a larger class of characters. We have several such symbols:

- (.) matches any character. This is a special character.
- (\d) matches any digit between 0-9. We've used an escape, \, to make an ordinary d into a special \d.
- (\s) matches any whitespace: spacebar, tab, newline, carriage return, form feed, or vertical tab. The first two, spacebar and tab, are pretty common. A newline is often only present at the end of a string, and sometimes we'll intentionally strip that. The other characters are really rare.
- (\w) matches any word character. Since this includes letters, digits, and the (_) character, it will match proper Python identifiers.

- [. . .] matches any character inside the brackets. We can use [wxyz] to match any character from the four characters listed explicitly. We can use [A-Z] to match any character in the range A to Z. We can use something like [a-zA-Z0-9_] to match ASCII word characters the hard way (\w is the easy way.) There are a few special cases for this:
  - To match a - character, we have to use it either first or last inside []. Something like this is not a good idea: [+-*/]. This is because there's an implied range of characters from + to *. However, [-+*/] works perfectly. Putting the – character first means it's no longer part of a range; it's just a hyphen.
  - To match a] character, we have to escape it with \].
  - Other special characters such as ., *, and so on, will lose their special meanings in this set specification.
- [^. . .] matches any character which is not in the given set. This is the inverse of [. . .].
- (\D) matches any non-digit character.
- (\S) matches any non-whitespace character; this will be either a punctuation character or a word character.
- (\W) matches any non-word character; this will be either a punctuation character or a whitespace character.

As an example, we can locate an hour:minute:second timestamp in a longer string using a pattern like r'\d\d:\d\d:\d\d'. This pattern will match an eight character string that has digits and punctuation in the given order.

Let's put this simple expression to use.

Finding a pattern in a file

Let's look at the simple problem of scanning a file for the occurrence of a specific pattern. We'll explore the basics and then scale our design for more complex patterns. For our initial exploration, we don't even really need to process a file. We can leverage the idea that Python has a large variety of file-like objects.

The first step in using a pattern is compiling it. The re module includes some functions that work directly with the pattern text. While these are handy, it's more efficient to compile a pattern explicitly and use the compiled version many times. When we're using pattern to match thousands (or millions) of lines of a file, small efficiencies like compiling a pattern add up quickly.

Here's how we compile a pattern:

```
>>> import re
>>> pattern = re.compile(r'\d\d:\d\d:\d\d')
>>> print(pattern)
re.compile('\\d\\d:\\d\\d:\\d\\d')
```

We've provided the regular expression as a raw string because it has six \ characters in it. The `re.compile()` function will translate the pattern string into an internal representation that's optimized for speedy examination of a block of text.

When we print a pattern object, it displays the code used to produce the pattern. Note that the printed output shows the pattern string in Python's preferred canonical string notation. Instead of showing a raw string, it shows a non-raw (cooked) Python string. Because \ is Python's escape character, it uses \\ to stand for a single \ in the resulting string object.

> **Raw versus cooked strings**
>
> Raw strings, for example, `r'stuff with \b in it'`, are untouched by Python. No replacement happens.
>
> Cooked strings, such as `'stuff with \b in it'`, use \ to escape the meaning of the next character. This means that all \x escape sequences are replaced by characters. \unnnn, for example, is replaced by the Unicode character with the given number. \N{name} is replaced by a Unicode character with the given name. There are several short escapes, including \n, \r, \t, \f, \v, and \b, which translate to various kinds of whitespace characters in the resulting string object.

Once we have the pattern object, we can use it to match source text. There are several ways to look for a regular expression pattern in source text:

- **Finding**: This will find all occurrences in the given text. We can use `pattern.findall()` and `pattern.finditer()` for this.
- **Searching**: This will find one occurrence somewhere in a string. We'll use `pattern.search()` for this.
- **Matching**: This will determine if the entire source string matches the pattern. We use `pattern.match()` and `pattern.fullmatch()`.
- **Splitting**: This will use the pattern to break the source text into sections. We use `pattern.split()` for this.
- **Substitution**: This will replace occurrences of the pattern with another pattern. We use `pattern.sub()` and `pattern.subn()` for this.

Tracks, Trails, and Logs

Here's an example of finding all occurrences in a long string:

```
some_text = """
This is a sample block of text
It starts at 06:41:15.
And it has non-matching rows.
It ends at 06:42:23.
"""

def find_times_in(text):
    pattern = re.compile(r'\d\d:\d\d:\d\d')
    for match in pattern.finditer(text):
        print(match)
```

First, we defined a long string using triple quotes (`"""`), and saved it in the `some_text` variable. In later examples, we'll show how to read the string from a file, or from a URL on the Internet. For now, we'll stick with a literal.

Second, we defined a function that will compile a pattern, and the find all matches of that pattern in the source string. We're using the `finditer()` method of the pattern object. We provide a block of sample text to this method of the pattern. The pattern object will then sweep through the text, yielding each match.

The `finditer()` method collaborates with the `for` statement. Each individual `Match` object created by the `finditer()` method is assigned to the `match` variable. In this example, we're merely printing the `Match` objects.

When we run this, we'll see an output that looks like this:

```
>>> find_times_in(some_text)
<_sre.SRE_Match object; span=(50, 58), match='06:41:15'>
<_sre.SRE_Match object; span=(101, 109), match='06:42:23'>
```

The output shows the two match objects. The default string representation of a match object shows the span of characters which matched, and it also shows the actual text which matched.

To work with the text which matched, we use the `group()` method of a `Match` object. We can define a slightly more useful function like this:

```
def all_times_in(text):
    pattern = re.compile(r'\d\d:\d\d:\d\d')
    return [x.group() for x in pattern.finditer(text)]
```

This function uses the same pattern object, but it creates a list of all of the places where the text was found. This last is built using a technique called a comprehension: we've embedded a `for` loop as a generator expression inside the brackets `[]` that mark the list. The generator expression uses the `finditer()` method to create a sequence of `Match` objects. Each `Match` object is assigned to a variable, `x`, the value of `x.group()` is the group of characters which matched the pattern.

The output from this function is a list of groups of characters which match the pattern. It looks like this:

```
['06:41:15', '06:42:23']
```

We've extracted two pieces of data from a larger block of text. We're able to do this without worrying about details of the larger block of text.

It turns out that this is so common that each pattern has a method which does this for us. The `findall()` method returns a list of the matched text. We can use `pattern.findall(text)` to get a list of text items, and we can use the more general `list(pattern.finditer(text))` method to get a list of `Match` objects.

Using regular expression suffix operators

So far, we looked at regular expression symbols that stand for any character from a larger set. We can use `r'\d'`, for example, to match for any digit character; we could also use `r'[0-9]'`. Other useful regular expression features are the suffixes that we can use to express repetition. This can include a finite number of repeats, but it also includes an indefinite number of repeats.

We have several forms of suffixes:

- (`*`): The previous regular expression can be repeated any number of times. This includes zero repetitions, which means the previous expression is optional. This is the greedy version; it has to be used carefully with generic patterns. If we write `r'.*\d'` to match some characters followed by a digit, we'll be unhappy because the greedy `.*` will also match the digit.

- (`*?`): The previous regular expression can be repeated any number of times. This is the non-greedy version; when used with generic patterns like `.`; this will stop matching as early as possible. If we write `r'.*?\d'` to match some characters followed by a digit, the non-greedy `.*?` will stop matching when it reaches the digit.

- (`+`): The previous expression can be repeated one or more times. This is the greedy version.

[41]

Tracks, Trails, and Logs

- (+?): This is the non-greedy version that matches one or more characters.

- (?): The previous expression is optional; it can be repeated zero or one time only.

- {x}: The previous expression must be repeated *x* times.

- {x,y}: The previous expression must be repeated between *x* and *y* times. We can think of ? as short-hand for the equivalent {0,1}.

We can also use () to group expressions so that something rather complex can be repeated. We actually have several different varieties of () available to us.

- Simple (*pattern*) will both group regular expressions together and also capture the matching text within the group. We can use the match.group() method to return the captured text.

- The more ornate (?:*pattern*) will group regular expressions together, but won't capture the details. We use these like this: r'(?:\d\d:){2}(?:\d\d)'. Note that the (?: construct is just a long-winded three-character version of a). The regular expression inside the parenthesis includes \d\d:; the colon is a character that must be found after two digits. When reading this kind of code, we have to mentally isolate (?: and the following) as punctuation around \d\d:.

A common file format is a properties file. This will have lines that include a name, some punctuation (either : or =), and a value. A properties file might look like this:

```
time_of_day = 06:00
map_zone =   amz117
synopsis = amz101
```

We can parse these lines with a pattern like that looks like this:

```
r'\w+\s*[=:]\s*.*'
```

Let's break this down carefully. We'll use the verbose mode to write lots of extra details about the pattern we're defining. In verbose mode, actual spaces in the pattern (as well as # comments) are ignored. This lets us write comments to clarify how a pattern works. Here's an example:

```
>>> prop_pat_v = re.compile(
... r'''\w+ # A-Za-z0-9_ repeated
...     \s*   # 0 or more spaces
...     [=:]  # punctuation
...     \s*   # 0 or more spaces
...     .*    # Anything
...     ''', re.VERBOSE )
```

[42]

We've annotated the interesting pieces of the regular expression to clarify how we'll match items. We've used a mixture of character class symbols, including \w, \s, and .. We've used the + suffix to match one or more characters of the \w class. We've used the .* construct to match an indefinite number of characters.

Here's where the () characters for grouping come into play. We can use the () symbols to separate the label from the value:

```
>>> prop_pat_g = re.compile( r'(\w+)\s*[=:]\s*(.*)', )
>>> for match in prop_pat_g.finditer( properties_file ):
...     print( match.group(1), match.group(2) )
time_of_day 06:00
map_zone amz117
synopsis amz101
```

We've introduced () around \w+ to capture the label and around .* to capture the value. We're using plain () because we want the matched characters to be available as match.group(1) and match.group(2).

Capturing characters by name

The core feature of wrapping a regular expression in () to capture matching characters is really useful. It allows us to parse a complex string into the relevant pieces. Because we can use indefinite matching, like \s+ and \s*, we can tolerate flexible whitespace, allowing a person to format their input any way they want to.

The one downside of taking the groups of characters apart is remembering which group number has which piece of the overall string. With a simple two-item pattern for parsing a properties file, it's pretty easy to remember what group(1) and group(2) both mean. For more complex data formats, this can become a source of errors.

The regular expression language has a third kind of () for collecting matched characters:

(?P<name>pattern)

This allows us to provide a name for the characters that are captured and match the pattern. We can get the characters using match.group('name'), which is very similar to the match.group(number) method that we've already used.

Tracks, Trails, and Logs

This leads us to the following kind of function to parse the text read from a properties file:

```
def properties(text):
    prop_pat_named = re.compile( r'(?P<key>\w+)\s*[=:]\
s*(?P<value>.*)', )
    prop_dict= {}
    for match in prop_pat_named.finditer( properties_file ):
        prop_dict[match.group('key')]= match.group('value')
    return prop_dict
```

We've created yet another variation on our regular expression. In this example, we've used named groups, bracketed with the (?P<*name*> *some pattern*) parenthesis. We've also initialized the `prop_dict` variable with an empty dictionary object. The `for` statement will iterate through all the matching property settings.

For each match in the block of text, we'll extract characters to act as key and value. We'll use the matching characters named `key` in the regular expression to be the key in our properties dictionary. We'll use the matching characters called `value` in the regular expression to be the value for that key.

When we evaluate this function on a block of text, it might look like this:

```
>>> properties(properties_file)
{'time_of_dany': '06:00', 'map_zone': 'amz117', 'synopsis': 'amz101'}
```

We've use the properties example text from the previous section as the `properties_file` variable. The properties function located all name and value pairs, loaded a dictionary, and returned the resulting dictionary object. We've grabbed data from a file using regular expressions and created a useful data structure with that data.

Because of the flexibility built into our regular expressions, a few extra spaces or blank lines in the file will have no impact on the resulting dictionary. Regular expressions allow us to create a lot of flexibility in our Python applications.

Looking at the CLF

The basic definition of Apache CLF is available at `http://httpd.apache.org/docs/2.4/mod/mod_log_config.html#formats`.

Based on this specification, we can see that a web log will have at least seven fields. Some typical lines might look like this:

```
109.128.44.217 - - [31/May/2015:22:55:59 -0400] "GET / HTTP/1.1"
200 14376 "-" "Mozilla/5.0 (iPad; CPU OS 8_1_2 like Mac OS X)
AppleWebKit/600.1.4 (KHTML, like Gecko) Version/8.0 Mobile/12B440
```

```
Safari/600.1.4"
109.128.44.217 - - [31/May/2015:22:56:00 -0400] "GET /_static/default.
css HTTP/1.1" 200 4040 "http://buildingskills.itmaybeahack.com/"
"Mozilla/5.0 (iPad; CPU OS 8_1_2 like Mac OS X) AppleWebKit/600.1.4
(KHTML, like Gecko) Version/8.0 Mobile/12B440 Safari/600.1.4"
109.128.44.217 - - [31/May/2015:22:56:00 -0400] "GET /_images/
Cover3x4.jpg HTTP/1.1" 200 15986 "http://buildingskills.
itmaybeahack.com/" "Mozilla/5.0 (iPad; CPU OS 8_1_2 like Mac OS X)
AppleWebKit/600.1.4 (KHTML, like Gecko) Version/8.0 Mobile/12B440
Safari/600.1.4"
```

We can see the following fields described in the CLF definition:

- `host`: This is an IP address like `109.128.44.217`.

- `identity`: Generally, this is - unless the web server enforces authentication.

- `user`: Generally, this is – as well.

- `time`: This is a timestamp, `31/May/2015:22:56:00 -0400`, in `[]`. This has several subfields: day, month, year, hour, minute, second, and the offset from UTC time. We can use the `datetime` module to parse this.

- `request`: This is the actual HTTP request, `GET / HTTP/1.1`, surrounded by `"`. This has three parts—the method, the path to the resource, and the protocol that was used.

- `status`: This is the response from the server, often 200 to show success. It might be 404 for a page that's not found.

- `bytes`: This is the number of bytes transmitted. Sometimes, this is (-) if no page was returned.

- `referer`: This is a source for the request surrounded by `"`. In some cases, it might be - because it's not known or was explicitly concealed. In other cases, it will be the URL for a web page which contained a link that was followed to this page:

  Yes, "referer" is spelled wrong; this is a long-standing problem in the original Request For Comments used to define the protocol.

- `user_agent`: The software being used to browse the web, surrounded by `"`. In this case, it is an iPad running Safari. However, there are also a lot of additional details about the compatibility of the software and how the software was built.

Ideally, each field is simply separated by spaces. Some fields are complex and contain internal spaces, and so they're surrounded by `[]` or `"`. This leads to a longish regular expression to decompose the log entries.

[45]

Tracks, Trails, and Logs

Here's the pattern we can use, exploded out in verbose mode:

```
clf_pat= re.compile(r'''
    (?P<host>[\d\.]+)\s+        # Usually an IP Address
    (?P<identity>\S+)\s+        # Often -
    (?P<user>\S+)\s+            # Also -
    \[(?P<time>.+?)\]\s+        # [31/May/2015:22:55:59 -0400]
    "(?P<request>.+?)"\s+       # "GET / HTTP/1.1"
    (?P<status>\d+)\s+          # Status number
    (?P<bytes>\d+|-)\s+         # Number of bytes or "-"
    "(?P<referer>.*?)"\s+       # [SIC]
    "(?P<user_agent>.*?)"\s*    # The browser
    ''', re.VERBOSE )
```

In general, the fields are separated by one or more spaces: each field ends with `\s+`. The final field may not have any trailing spaces, so we've include `\s*` to match zero or more spaces at the end of the line.

Some fields in this pattern are matched very specifically, others use general patterns. In some cases, we use a pattern that's moderately specific. The pattern for host will match any number of `\d` and `\.`. This will match a typical IP address, but it will also match junk like `1.2.3...7.8.9`. We could use `(?:\d+\.){3}\d+` to specifically look for IPv4 addresses, but that will be too specific; we'd have to use a more complex `(?:[0-9a-f]+:){7}[0-9a-f]+` to match an IPv6 address for logs from systems that use the newer addresses. We could have used `\s+` to match anything that's not a space; this seems a bit too general.

In some cases, we've adopted a very general pattern. The identity and and user fields must use `\s+` to match anything which isn't a space. The time, request, user agent, and referer fields all use an even more general `.+?` to match anything without being too greedy. For time, the non-greedy `.+?` will stop matching at the `]`; for the other three fields, it will stop matching at the following `"` character.

The bytes field is matched using `\d+|-` to represent either many digits, `\d+`, or a single hyphen `-`. This uses the regular expression `or` operator, which is `|`.

Some log files are available in text mode and will be easy to read and process. Some log files, however, are compressed, using gzip. In order to make sense of these files, we'll need another Python library.

[46]

Chapter 2

Reading and understanding the raw data

Files come in a variety of formats. Even a file that appears to be simple text is often a UTF-8 encoding of Unicode characters. When we're processing data to extract intelligence, we need to look at three tiers of representation:

- Physical Format: We might have a text file encoded in UTF-8, or we might have a GZIP file, which is a compressed version of the text file. Across these different physical formats, we can find a common structure. In the case of log files, the common structure is a line of text which represents a single event.

- Logical Layout: After we've extracted data from the physical form, we often find that the order of the fields is slightly different or some optional fields are missing. The trick of using named groups in a regular expression gives us a way to handle variations in the logical layouts by using different regular expressions depending on the details of the layout.

- Conceptual Content: This is the data we were looking for, represented as proper Python objects. We can then do any analysis required on these meaningful objects.

To deal with these three tiers, we'll often write collections of functions so that we can mix and match as needed. We'll look at some physical format processing techniques first.

Our goal is to make the physical format of the file transparent to other parts of the analysis application. We'd like to be able to read a gzipped file with the same level of simplicity as we read a text file. In some cases, we merely need to replace the open() function to achieve some transparency. This doesn't always work, so it's easier to write a family of generator functions that yield lines allowing for unique features of a file format.

Our target function looks like this:

```python
def local_text_long(filename):
    with open(filename, "rt") as log:
        for line in log:
            yield line.rstrip()
```

This will generate all of the lines in a text file. We've used rt as the open mode, even though this is generally assumed. For other physical formats, this may not be the default assumption, and it helps to clarify this early and often. This function will remove the line ending character and any trailing whitespace, also.

[47]

Tracks, Trails, and Logs

We can use this generator function in a `for` loop like this:

```
>>> for line in local_text_long('buildingskills.itmaybeahack.com-
Jun-2015.log'):
...     match = clf_pat.match(line)
...     print(match.group('status'))
```

This produces 31,000 lines of status codes; not really useful output. To be more useful, we'd need to make a collection to summarize the data. Once we have a consistent way to handle `gzip` and text formats, we'll look into more useful analyses.

We're creating a generator function so that we don't have to place an entire log file in memory to process it. We're going to leverage an aspect of generator functions known as laziness. When we use a file object in a `for` loop, the file object is lazy about reading bytes and returning complete lines. Only enough data is read to return the next line of the file. The same principle holds for functions using a yield statement. One line of the file is read and one stripped line is yielded from the function. Memory use is optimized, allowing us to work with very, very large collections of data.

Reading a gzip compressed file

We want our function that reads from `gzip` files to look just like our function that reads text files. This will allow us to process either kind of file transparently. We can apply the concept of polymorphism—usually reserved for class definitions—to functions as well. Here's how we can read all the lines of a compressed version of a log file:

```
import gzip
def local_gzip(filename):
    with gzip.open(filename, "rt") as log:
        yield from (line.rstrip() for line in log)
```

The parameters to our `local_gzip()` function match the parameters to our `local_text_long()` function. We'll make sure that the results of these functions match so that either of them can be used to process a file.

Note that the `gzip` module's `open()` function requires us to explicitly state that we're reading the file in text mode. The `gzip` module can deal with a wide variety of files, and defaults to reading bytes instead of Unicode characters.

We've used the new `yield from` statement to yield all of the lines of the generator function without the overhead of explicitly writing a `for` statement. This `yield from` parallels the `for` and `yield` statements in the `local_text_long()` function.

[48]

We'll leave it to each agent to rewrite `local_text_long()` into `local_text()`. The new `local_text()` should have the same results as `local_text_long()`, but make use of the `yield from` statement.

Rather than simply print 31,000 rows of details, let's summarize a particular attribute. The host field provides the IP address of someone making a request. It's not a unique identifier because a router can make it appear that multiple individuals all have the same address. We'd need to look at cookies to try to track individual users.

We're using named groups in our pattern. This handles logical layout issues for us. We can analyze a specific column like this:

```
from collections import Counter
def common(limit=12):
    unique_ip = Counter()
    for line in local_gzip('buildingskills.itmaybeahack.com-Jun-2015.
gz'):
        match = clf_pat.match(line)
        if match is None:
            print( line )
            continue
        unique_ip[match.group('host')] += 1
    return unique_ip.most_common(limit)
```

We're using the `Counter` class from the `collections` module to summarize the raw data into something we can report back to headquarters.

Our function creates an empty `Counter` and assigns this to the `unique_ip` variable. As we read each row of a log, we'll use the `clf_pat.match()` method to try and create a `Match` object. If the `clf_pat` pattern can't create a `Match` object, it means that our pattern doesn't properly describe a specific line of data. We'll need to see the line and correct our pattern.

The `Match` object is assigned to a variable with the unimaginative name of `match`. The `match.group()` method will return any of the named groups. The characters captured by `match.group('host')` will be the IP address making the request. We use this string to update the `Counter` object assigned to the `unique_ip` variable.

The final result is the most common IP addresses that are making requests for this web site. We'll need to do some additional processing to find out who owns the IP address. It's time-consuming to do this resolution, so we'll set it aside for now.

Tracks, Trails, and Logs

Reading remote files

We've given these functions names such as `local_text` and `local_gzip` because the files are located on our local machine. We might want to write other variations that use `urrlib.request.urlopen()` to open remote files. For example, we might have a log file on a remote server that we'd like to process. This allows us to write a generator function, which yields lines from a remote file allowing us to interleave processing and downloading in a single operation.

We can use the `urllib.request` module to handle remote files using URLs of this form: `ftp://username:password@/server/path/to/file`. We can also use URLs of the form `file:///path/to/file` to read local files. Because of this transparency, we might want to look at using `urllib.request` for all file access.

As a practical matter, it's somewhat more common to use FTP to acquire files in bulk.

Studying a log in more detail

A file is the serialized representation for Python objects. In some rare cases, the objects are strings, and we can deserialize the strings from the text file directly. In the case of our web server logs, some of the strings represent a date-time stamp. Also, the size of the transmitted content shouldn't be treated as a string, since it's properly either an integer size or the None object if nothing was transmitted to the browser.

When requests for analysis come in, we'll often have to convert objects from strings to more useful Python objects. Generally, we're happiest if we simply convert everything into a useful, native Python data structure.

What kind of data structure should we use? We can't continue to use a `Match` object: it only knows about strings. We want to work with integers and datetimes.

The first answer is often to create a customized class that will hold the various attributes from a single entry in a log. This gives the most flexibility. It may, however, actually be more than we need. We can also collect distinct data items into a `namedtuple` object. The `collections` module has a `namedtuple` function that introduces a new class into our application. This allows us to access individual attributes by name, but we don't have to write a complete class definition.

We can also do this with a `SimpleNamespace` object. This comes from the `types` module. This offers more flexibility; that flexibility introduces a cost of more storage than a `namedtuple`. A `SimpleNamespace` object is even simpler than creating a `namedtuple` object, so we'll start there.

Chapter 2

We can create a `SimpleNamespace` object by assigning names and values in the constructor. We can do things like this:

```
>>> from types import SimpleNamespace
>>> options = SimpleNamespace(
...     time_of_day = '06:00',
...     map_zone = 'amz117',
...     synopsis = 'amz101' )
```

We've created a `SimpleNamespace` object and assigned it to the options variable. The reason we like to use a `SimpleNamespace` object is we've created a collection of named attributes. We can now manipulate this object with code that looks like this:

```
>>> options.map_zone
'amz117'
```

The `SimpleNamespace` object is a Python object with named attributes but no customized method functions. For these kinds of statistical and analytical applications, this kind of object is ideal.

Using the `**` operator, we can populate a `SimpleNamespace` object from a dictionary. A regular expression `Match` object has a `groupdict()` method, which produces a dictionary of named groups. If we make sure that our group names are valid Python identifiers, we can easily build a `SimpleNamespace` object directly from valid matches.

We'll need a function that can take the output from a `local_gzip()` or `local_text()` function, and create `SimpleNamespace` instances. The code looks like this:

```
from types import SimpleNamespace
import datetime
def log_event_1(line_iter):
    for line in line_iter:
        match= clf_pat.match(line)
        event= SimpleNamespace( **match.groupdict() )
        event.datetime= datetime.datetime.strptime(
            event.time, "%d/%b/%Y:%H:%M:%S %z")
        event.bytes= None if event.bytes == '-' else int(event.bytes)
        yield event
```

The argument to this function must be a line iterator that provides clean lines from some kind of log file. We'll match those lines using our `clf_pat` pattern. We'll then build a `SimpleNamespace` object from the `groupdict()` dictionary that has each group name and each group string as its value.

[51]

Tracks, Trails, and Logs

Once we have this `SimpleNamespace` object, we can tweak the attributes. We'll make two significant changes in this function. First, we'll throw in an additional attribute, `datetime`, which contains a proper `datetime` object. Second, we'll replace the `bytes` attribute with either a `None` object or a proper integer value.

We can make a strong case for always adding new attributes and never replacing an existing attribute. This can simplify debugging because the original data is still present in the object. We can also make a strong case for replacing attributes where the original data isn't useful as a string. We've included both in this example to provide food for thought. There's no right answer, and experienced agents know that absolutes like never and always are always a source of confusion and should never be used.

Now we can easily refer to `event.host`, `event.datetime`, and `event.request`. This is even better than `match.group('request')`. Speaking of the request, this is a three-part field. We'll need to break this down, also, so that we can explore the path.

What are they downloading?

In order to see what people are downloading, we'll need to parse the `request` field. This field has three elements: a method, a path, and a protocol. The method is almost always `GET` and the protocol is almost always `HTTP/1.1`. The path, however, shows the resource which was requested. This tells us what people are reading from a given website.

In our case, we can expand on the processing done in `log_event_1()` to gather the path information. It's a small change, and we'll add this line:

```
        event.method, event.path, event.protocol = event.request.
    split(" ")
```

This will update the event object by splitting the `event.request` attribute to create three separate attributes: `event.method`, `event.path`, and `event.protocol`.

We'll leave it to each individual agent to create the `log_event_2()` function from their `log_event_1()` function. It's helpful to have sample data and some kind of simple unit test to be sure that this works. We can use this `log_event_2()` function as follows:

```
>>> unique_paths = Counter(
...     event.path for event in log_event_2( local_gzip(filename) ) )
>>> unique_paths.most_common(20)
```

[52]

We've created a `Counter` object based on all of the `event.path` attribute values that are returned from the `log_event_2()` function. Since the `log_event_2()` function includes the additional step of parsing the request, we can depend on the presence of the `path` attribute in each event object.

Within the top 20 paths, we can see items like these:

- `2161 /favicon.ico`
- `170 /robots.txt`
- `163 /`

We've printed the value (the count of occurrences) and the key for three items. The 2,161 requests for the `favicon.ico` file show how many users retrieve any of the HTML page. The site has PDF files and other downloads; this shows us that downloads are much more popular than the HTML content. Of the HTML requests, 170 were clearly requests that hit the `robots.txt` file. The `robots.txt` file is used to steer tools like Google around the site when doing indexing. 163 requests where for the top-level / path, which usually returns the home page, `index.html`. The other 1,998 requests were for some HTML deeper inside the site.

Trails of activity

We can leverage the referrer (famously misspelled *referer*) information to track access around a web site. As with other interesting fields, we need to decompose this into host name and path information. The most reliable way to do this is to use the `urllib.parse` module.

This means that we'll need to make a change to our `log_event_2()` function to add yet another parsing step. When we parse the referrer URL, we'll get at least six pieces of information:

- `scheme`: This is usually `http`.
- `netloc`: This is the server which made the referral. This will be the name of the server, not the IP address.
- `path`: This is the path to the page which had the link.
- `params`: This can be anything after the ? symbol in a URL. Usually, this is empty for simple static content sites.
- `fragment`: This can be anything after the # in a URL.

[53]

Tracks, Trails, and Logs

These details are items within a `Namedtuple` object: we can refer to them by name or by position within the tuple. We have three ways to handle the parsing of URLs:

- We can simply put the `Namedtuple` object into our `SimpleNamespace` object. To get the host that sent a referral, we'd use something like `event.referer.netloc`.

We can put all six things into separate named fields in the `SimpleNamespace` object. This would lead to a small problem with the name path, because we have a path we extracted from the request, as well as a path extract from the referer. To get the host that sent a referral, we'd use something like `event.netloc`.

- We can be really slick and convert the `namedtuple` object into a `SimpleNamespace` object. While this is a cool use of the `vars()` function, it leads to syntax that looks like option 1. It doesn't seem to be adding significant value.

We'll call our new function `log_event_3()`; it will be based on `log_event_2()`, but it will have this line inserted:

```
event.referer = urllib.parse.urlparse(event.referer)
```

Now, we can do the following analysis to see who our top referrers are:

```
>>> unique_referer_host = Counter(
...         event.referer.netloc for event in log_event_3(local_
gzip(filename)) )
>>> unique_referer_host
```

There are two interesting bits of information in this output. First, we can see that 19,479 referrers are internal references from page to page within the web site. From this, we can see what a person clicked next as they browsed. This can be a very interesting analysis.

Second, we can see that 33 references are from completely outside the site. Places like `www.couponmate.com` apparently have a link to this site. Since only one of these links was followed, that means there might be some opportunities left on the table. Perhaps the owner of the site needs to reach out to make some better sales and marketing relationships with these sites that are acting as referrers.

Chapter 2

Who is this person?

We can learn more about an IP address using the Whois program. For agents with Linux or Mac OS X, the Whois program is built-in. Agents using Windows may want to download and install a whois program. See `https://technet.microsoft.com/en-us/sysinternals/bb897435.aspx` for more information.

The Whois program will examine the various registries used to track the names of servers on the internet. It will provide whatever information is available for a given server. This often includes the name of a person or organization that owns the server.

We'll start by using the built-in whois program. An alternative is to make a REST API request to a whois service using `urllib`. We're going to defer making REST API requests to the *Chapter 3, Following the Social Network*.

The Whois program makes a request of a server and displays the results. The request is a single line of text, usually containing a domain name or IP address. The response from the server is a flood of text providing information about the server or address.

This particular request/response protocol dates from the early days of the internet; it was initially developed in 1982. It has seen some changes, but it's still a rather primitive tool. For more information, see `https://en.wikipedia.org/wiki/WHOIS`.

We can experiment with the Whois program from the command line by running a command like this:

```
$ whois 201.160.255.73
```

This will dump a great deal of information about the IP address given in the query. The exact source of the data varies based on the agent's location and OS configuration. For agents based in the US, this will generally start with `whois.arin.net` to do the actual work and respond appropriately.

We can get some additional information about the whois program by running the `whois ?` command. This will send the `?` query to the whois server, which may send back a summary of what information the server can provide.

Because this protocol has relatively unstructured definition, the format for the query and the nature of the responses are highly variable. Different servers can (and will) behave differently. There are some common patterns. Therefore, we'll need to use a very flexible design as we gather information the IP addresses hitting a given site.

Tracks, Trails, and Logs

Clearly, we don't want to run the `whois` command-line program manually to gather information about users. We want to have this automated. Note that we'll run into problems if we try to resolve every single IP address: most servers will throttle our requests. Rather than blindly make requests until we get an error, we can limit our exploration to the top few dozen users of a web site.

Using Python to run other programs

One of Python's strengths is its ability to run other programs that are already installed on our computer. We can do this with the `subprocess` module. This creates a child process that runs the given program. We can collect the output from that child process.

In this respect, Python is essentially another shell. It turns out that Python can do all of the things that the Korn shell (ksh) or the Bash shell do. A common Python trick is to include a `#!/usr/bin/env python3` line at the beginning of every `.py` script so that when the file is executed, the shell will hand the work off to Python seamlessly. Indeed, it's often easier to write shell-like programs in Python than in one of the traditional OS shells.

We can use the `os` module to have our Python program run other programs. The `os.spawn...()` family of functions, for example, will start another program, providing command-line options and environment variables. The complexity arises in setting up the internal file descriptors for the child process. Also, the Windows implementation is not thread-safe: a multi-threaded application will have problems. The Python Standard Library warns us away from casual use of the `os` module, and suggests we use the `subprocess` module.

We'll focus on the `check_output()` function of the `subprocess` module. This function will create a child process, wait for it to finish, and gather the output from that child. We need to provide the name of the program we want to run, and any of the command-line arguments to that program.

We have two forms for the command that creates the child process:

- We can write the command as a single string to be parsed by the OS's shell (`bash` or `cmd.exe`). This is very flexible but involves the overhead of actually running the shell which then runs the target program.

- We can write the command as a sequence of strings as if the shell had already done the parsing. This requires a bit more care, since we don't have all of the cool features of the shell.

[56]

Since our needs are relatively simple, we'll stick with the second option. We can submit a command like this:

```
>>> import subprocess
>>> command = ['pwd']
>>> subprocess.check_output(command).decode("utf-8")
```

We've created a command that's a very short sequence with a single string in it. Windows Agents can use the `chdir` (or `cd`) command instead of the Linux **pwd** command as something that reports a single, easy-to-understand result.

We send the list of strings to the OS to be executed. The output will be a stream of bytes, which we can then decode to recover Unicode characters.

We can use something like `['echo', 'some confirmation string']` as an example of a slightly more complex command.

An interesting difference between POSIX operating systems (Mac OS X and Linux) and Windows is the way wild-cards are handled. A Windows agent can use `['ls', '*.py']` as a command, and get an interesting result that shows many files. Mac OS X and Linux don't handle wild-cards this way: they're handled by the shell, long before the actual command is executed. For this to work in Mac OS X or Linux, we'd have to add the `shell=True` keyword parameter.

Processing whois queries

The `whois` command requires an IP address. It may need to include a specific **Network Information Center (NIC)** host name. We might, for example, need to use the `whois.lacnic.net` to resolve address owned in **Latin America or Caribbean (LAC)**.

We'll need a function that can build two forms of the `whois` command. One form will use our default host, and the other will allow us to plugin a specific host.

Here's one way to handle this:

```
import subprocess
def get_whois(ip, server=None):
    command = ["whois"]
    if server:
        command.extend(["-h", server])
    command.append(ip)
    results= subprocess.check_output(command).decode("us-ascii")
    return results.splitlines()
```

[57]

Tracks, Trails, and Logs

Our function starts by building the command as a list of strings. We've used a generic name for the command. If this is run in a context where the PATH environment variable has been altered dramatically, an unexpected whois program might get executed; where this is a concern, using /usr/bin/whois avoids this potential problem.

If we have been given a specific server to use, we'll append two more strings to the command. We'll put the target IP address last. Once we've built the sequence of strings, we can then execute the whois command, collect the output, and then decode Unicode characters from the sequence of bytes.

In the case of whois command, the encoding is often ASCII, not UTF-8. The standard RFC 3912 (https://tools.ietf.org/html/rfc3912) is clear that the encoding is not itself standardized: some sleuth work may be required to decode the character set used by a particular host.

We've split the result into lines because this seems helpful for initial exploration. In the long run, this may not really be the best idea. It will be much more helpful to split the output into two tiers:

- A stanza that separated from other stanzas by completely blank lines. Some stanzas have comments marked with # or %. Some stanzas have name: value lines. Some of the names are unique, but some names are repeated in different stanzas; therefore, each stanza has to be treated as a distinct object.

- A line within a stanza. The content of the line depends on the type of stanza: this will either be a comment line or an individual name: value pair.

Also, the Whois program can actually accept an indefinite number of IP addresses to resolve. We should define a function that will make all of our IP resolution requests in a single burst of activity.

Breaking a request into stanzas and lines

How can we decompose a list of strings into a collection of stanzas? How can we locate the blank lines that separate stanzas?

We have two general approaches. One way to do this is to index the blank lines. Any gap in the index numbers is a stanza. Let's say our response from whois command is a list of lines in the response variable. We can use a list comprehension to enumerate the indices of the blank lines:

```
blank_lines = [n for n, line in enumerate(response) if len(line) == 0]
```

[58]

This will produce the list of index positions where the length of the line is zero. The list will look like this:

```
[0, 8, 9, 16, 21, 33, 34, 35, 46, 47, 53, 59, 60, 68]
```

This tells us which lines separate the stanzas. We can pair these up to see where the stanzas begin and end. For example lines in the ranges 1-8, 10-16, 22-33, 36-46, and so on, are going to be the stanzas of non-blank lines.

How can we pair them up? We can use the `zip()` function to create pairs of numbers from two copies of the original list of blank lines:

```
start_end = zip( blank_lines[:-1], blank_lines[1:] )
```

This will take a copy of the `blank_lines` list without the very last value, and a copy of the `blank_lines` list that skips the very first value. We'll pair up items from both lists to create a dumb list of pairs of blank line indices. It looks like this:

```
[(0, 8), (8, 9), (9, 16), (16, 21), (21, 33), (33, 34), (34, 35), (35,
46), (46, 47), (47, 53), (53, 59), (59, 60), (60, 68)]
```

We can call this a dumb list because the sequence of lines from 8 to 9 will only have one line (line number 8) in it, and this line (by definition) is blank. Looking at this list again, note that the starting line in each pair is a blank line. The pair `(9, 16)` represents a stanza with the first line of meaningful text on line 10 and ending just before line 16. This means that we only want `(start, end)` pairs where `start+1 < end`.

This leads us to the third line of code in this process:

```
stanzas = [response[s+1:e] for s,e in start_end if s+1 < e]
```

We've picked ranges of lines from the response list. We've used the start-end pairs, but only when the range of lines between start and end will actually include some useful data.

These three lines are the body of a `split_stanzas()` function. We'll leave it to the field agents to assemble a working function out of these three lines.

Once we've decomposed the data into stanzas, we can identify the kind of stanza by looking at the first character of the first line. If it's # or %, we have some kind of comment or annotation block. Otherwise, we have a block that will require a pattern like `r'\w+:\s*\w+'` to extract the meaningful details.

[59]

Tracks, Trails, and Logs

Alternate stanza-finding algorithm

A second way to decompose a long list of text into stanzas is to use a generator function which buffers each stanza. The idea is that we can accumulate a list of non-blank lines and yield the whole block when we encounter a blank line.

The entire function looks like this:

```
def split_stanzas_2(response):
    stanza= []
    for line in response:
        if len(line) == 0:
            if stanza: yield stanza
            stanza= []
        else:
            stanza.append(line)
    if stanza: yield stanza
```

We've initialized an empty list and assigned it to the `stanza` variable. We'll use this to accumulate the lines of a stanza. We'll then use each line in the response object.

A blank line signals the end of a stanza. If we've accumulated any lines, we can yield the complete stanza. We can then reset the `stanza` variable to an empty list. A non-blank line is simply appended to the current stanza.

When we've exhausted the lines, we might have a complete stanza in our buffer. We need to yield this final stanza. While it seems like the output almost always ends with a blank line, we need to be sure to check the final status of the `stanza` variable, and yield a non-empty stanza.

Since this function is a generator, it works very nicely with the `for` statement. We can easily process each stanza to accumulate the relevant details about an IP address that's creating web traffic.

Making bulk requests

We can make two tiny tweaks to the `get_whois()` function that will allow us to get information about a list of IP addresses instead of a single address. The first change is to allow an unlimited number of `ip` parameters by using the `*` prefix on the positional parameter to this function:

```
def get_whois_2(*ip, server=None):
```

All argument values will be collected into a single list. If we need to provide a separate server address, we must use a keyword argument.

Chapter 2

Once we have a list of addresses, we change `append()` to `extend()` like this:

```
command.extend(ip)
```

Now all of the provided address will extend the command list. These two changes allow us to do the following kind of request:

```
get_whois_2('66.249.69.78', '201.160.255.73')
```

This will make in inquiry about a batch of IP addresses in a single request.

Getting logs from a server with ftplib

When we've created an analysis that HQ finds useful, we'll often have to scale this up to work on a larger supply of log files. This will involve acquiring and downloading files from servers without manually clicking a link to download and save each file.

We'll provide a sample of how we might use Python's `ftplib` to acquire files in bulk for analysis. Once we have the files locally, we can process them using our `local_gzip()` or `local_text()` functions.

Here's a function that performs a complex of FTP interaction:

```
import ftplib
def download( host, path, username=None ):
    with ftplib.FTP(host, timeout=10) as ftp:

        if username:
            password = getpass.getpass("Password: ")
            ftp.login(user=username,passwd=password)
        else:
            ftp.login()

        ftp.cwd(path)
        for name, facts in ftp.mlsd(".", ["type","size"]):
            if name.startswith("."): continue
            if facts['type'] == 'dir': continue
            print("Fetching", name, facts)
            command= "RETR {0}".format(name)
            with open(os.path.join(path,name), 'wb') as target:
                ftp.retrbinary(command, target.write)
        ftp.quit()
```

[61]

Tracks, Trails, and Logs

Our function needs four parameters: the host we're going to interact with, a path to the files, the username, and the password. We don't like the idea of passwords being handled casually, so we use the `getpass` module to prompt for a password. The `getpass.getpass()` function is like the `input()` function, but it will suppress echoing the characters on the console.

We've wrapped all the operations in a `with` statement because the FTP object is a context manager. Using the `with` statement assures us that all the network connections are dropped when we're done doing downloads. Even if an exception is raised, the FTP object will be able to close all of the connections before the exception handling starts.

We've broken this into two parts: authentication and download. The authentication part is used if there's a username. It will prompt for the password and provide these credentials to the FTP server via the `login()` method. If there's no username provided, we're doing a guest login via an empty `login()` request.

The `cwd()` method changes the working directory to the path given as an argument. We might have to change to a `logs` directory to locate web logs. Once we've changed directories, we'll use (`.`) for the local directory.

The `mlsd()` method provides a sequence of two-tuples. The first item of each tuple is the name of a file; the second item is a dictionary of the requested additional details. Filenames that begin with (`.`) are politely ignored by some OS; we follow this convention by skipping over these. We also skip over sub-directories by checking the content of the `facts` dictionary to see what type of file it is.

The actual download requires us to build a command and then use `retrbinary()` or `retrlines()` to initiate the command. The second argument to a `retr...()` method is a function which will be called for each block of data being transferred. We've used an inner `with` statement to act as a context manager for the target file; we assign the open file to the `target` variable. We can then provide the `target.write` function to be called for each block of data received from the server.

Building a more complete solution

A more complete solution could be something like this:

1. Download the current directory listing from a server, and save the details in a local file. If we create a simple list object, we can use the `pickle` module to save that list of information. We can also save a list of file information using the `json` module.

[62]

2. Compare the most recent download of directory information with the previous download of directory information. If they differ, we have a new file to analyze. If they're the same, there's nothing new to learn here.

3. For each changed file, download the raw file so that a `local_gzip()` or `local_text()` function can be used for analysis of the file. In most situations, we'll want to preserve the parsed data using the `csv` module to create an easy-to-process file that can be read without the overheads of processing regular expressions. This refined log data can now be examined efficiently since it's all local and all in simple `csv` notation.

4. The various kinds of analyses of most common IP addresses, most common downloads, most common referrers, and so on, can now be done on the cleaned-up, easy-to-parse `csv` files.

We'll leave it to each field agent to examine the `pickle`, `json`, and `csv` modules to locate ways to store local data that reflects the cleaned and parsed log files.

Summary

In this chapter, we discussed a large number of elements of data analysis. We've looked at how we have to disentangle physical format from logical layout and conceptual content. We covered the `gzip` module as an example of how we can handle one particularly complex physical format issue.

We focused a lot of attention on using the `re` module to write regular expressions that help us parse complex text files. This addresses a number of logical layout considerations. Once we've parsed the text, we can then do data conversions to create proper Python objects so that we have useful conceptual content.

We also saw how we can use a `collections.Counter` object to summarize data. This helps us find the most common items, or create complete histograms and frequency tables.

The `subprocess` module helped us run the whois program to gather data from around the internet. The general approach to using subprocess allows us to leverage a number of common utilities for getting information about the internet and the **World Wide Web**. For Windows agents, some of these utilities must be downloaded and installed since they're not available by default.

In the next chapter, we'll take a radically different approach to gathering intelligence. We'll look at the social network: the web of connections people form through online services. This will require us to make RESTful API requests from some of the social media web sites. We can learn quite a bit from how people are interacting and what they're saying to each other.

[63]

Following the Social Network

3

Intelligence gathering is really networking. It's networking with an avowed purpose of learning something new. It's an essentially social game. Most agents have connections; the more successful agents seem to have the most connections. When you read historical accounts of the British MI5/SIS agent code-named Garbo, you'll see how a vast and sophisticated social network is essential to espionage.

We'll leverage Twitter to gather pictures and text. We'll explore the Twitter Application Program Interface (API) to see what people are doing. The Twitter API uses Representational State Transfer (REST) as its protocol. We'll use Python's `http.client` to connect with RESTful web services like Twitter.

We can use the Twitter APIs to discover the extent of a social network. We'll try to discern the interactions one person has. We can use this to find the active connections among people. It requires some statistical care, but we can make steps toward discerning who leads and who follows. We can see some of what they're sharing.

In *Chapter 1, New Missions, New Tools*, we downloaded the necessary libraries to be able to process images and access Twitter. We'll make extensive use of the Twitter API package.

We'll be able to answer two important questions: Who's talking? What are they saying?

In this chapter, we'll be looking at the following topics:

- Introduction to image processing as a prelude to looking at social media
- How Pillow helps us examine image files safely and avoid the potential problems of viruses embedded in image files
- Using the Twitter API to see who's posting on Twitter

[65]

Following the Social Network

- Finding the followers of a given Twitter user (for some people, this is a small list; for others it can run to millions of names)
- Checking tweets and images attached to tweets
- Natural Language Tool Kit (NLTK)

The NLTK can be used to analyze the text of tweets. We won't dwell on this, since it's a very deep and complex subject. With these tools, we'll be able to examine social connections among the agents in our network.

Background briefing – images and social media

We'll use the Pillow implementation of the `PIL` package to extract and convert any graphics or images. In *Chapter 1, New Missions, New Tools*, we used the **pip3.4** program to install Pillow 2.9.0. The `PIL` package has modules that allow us to convert images to a common format. It also allows us to create thumbnails of images. This can help us build a tidy summary of images we collected.

Most importantly, it allows us to validate an image file. It turns out that the compression algorithms used on some images can be hacked. Someone can tweak the bytes of an image so that it appears to be infinitely large. This will cause the computer opening the image to get progressively slower until the image processing application finally crashes. A basic counter-intelligence ploy is to circulate damaged image files that leave agents struggling to figure out what went wrong.

The PIL module is an important piece of counter-counter-intelligence. We don't want to accept fraudulent or malicious files. The rule is simple: if we can't process the image in `PIL`, it's not a proper image file and should be discarded.

We'll start by grabbing some images from Flickr, since that's a good source of high-quality images, some of which are free from copyright constraints:

- Here's a link to one of our favorite photo streams: `https://www.flickr.com/photos/sdasmarchives/`.
- Here's another link to some other classic photos: `https://www.flickr.com/search/?tags=americascup&license=7%2C9%2C10`.

We'll use Pillow to create a standardized PNG thumbnail of an image. We'll aim to create something small that we can embed in an e-mail.

[66]

The essence of working with PIL is to open and operate on an Image object. PIL offers large number of functions and classes that we can use to transform or even create an image. We'll focus on the Image class itself in this introductory briefing.

Here's how we can create a properly scaled thumbnail image:

```
import os
from PIL import Image
def thumbnail(filename, target_max=128):
    name, ext = os.path.splitext( filename )
    thumb_name = name + "_thumb" + ".png"
    im = Image.open(filename)
    h, w = im.size
    scale = target_max / min(h, w)
    im.thumbnail( (h*scale, w*scale) )
    im.save(thumb_name, "PNG")
```

We defined a function that accepts a filename and a target maximum dimension. For images that are in portrait mode (*height > width*), this will specify the new height. For images that are in landscape mode (*width > height*), this will specify the new width.

We used the os.path.splitext() function to separate the filename from the extension. This allows us to append _thumb to the filename. We also switched the extension to .png because we're going to convert the image to PNG format.

The image-related processing starts when we open the Image. If the file is corrupt, damaged, or incomplete, this will raise an exception. If the file contains a hacked image, a warning is raised. If we want to treat this warning as an error and stop processing the file, we can use the warnings module. We would add this to our application in a global context:

```
warnings.simplefilter('error', Image.DecompressionBombWarning)
```

This line of code will escalate the warning into an error.

The im.size attribute has the height and width of the image. We can then determine the largest dimension, and compute the scaling factor from this. Since we're using exact division, we'll get a floating-point result. PIL automatically converts the floats to integers to determine the resulting size in pixels. The thumbnail() method of the image to resize it down to the target size. Finally, we save the image file in PNG format.

This shows us the essence of image processing with the PIL package. We opened an image file, made a transformation, and saved the resulting file.

Accessing web services with urllib or http.client

We'll look at the basics of making a web services request so that it's clear how things work under the hood.

Many web APIs follow the REST design pattern. The overall approach is based on the **Hypertext Transfer Protocol (HTTP)**, the backbone of the **World Wide Web (WWW)**.

The REST pattern leverages the method, path, and header parts of the HTTP request. The HTTP methods (`post`, `get`, `put`, and `delete`) to implement the canonical create, retrieve, update, and delete (CRUD) operations. The path is used to identify a resource. Because the HTTP path is often viewed as a hierarchy, an organization may define its resources in a complex hierarchy. The headers may also include some additional information like security credentials, or the data representation which should be used.

As a practical matter, some big web services will require us to sign up and get an API Key. This is how the data providers track usage and determine if you're doing something that's billable. Many agents have a large collection of API keys for a large number of data sources. Some APIs are revenue sources for the host organization. As every agent knows, information has value.

We'll focus our efforts on open data, readily available from government agencies at many levels. We'll use the `data.gov` catalog as an example of basic RESTful API requests.

For information, start at `https://www.data.gov`. You may also want to bookmark the `http://ckan.org/developers/about-ckan/` pages, since the CKAN project is used to implement the services in `data.gov`.

Here's a function that we can use to get the list of available datasets:

```python
import urllib.request
import urllib.parse
import json
import pprint

def get_packages(query, start=0, rows=100):
    request= {'q': query, 'start': start, 'rows': rows}
    data_string = urllib.parse.quote(json.dumps(request)).
encode('utf-8')
```

```
    with urllib.request.urlopen(
            'http://catalog.data.gov/api/3/action/package_search',
            data_string) as response:
        assert response.code == 200, "Unexpected response {0}".
format(response.code)
        response_dict = json.loads(response.read().decode('utf-8'))
    assert response_dict['success'], "Failed request {0}".
format(response)
    print( "Total Available", response_dict['result']['count'] )
    for item in response_dict['result']['results']:
        print( item['name'] )
```

We used two modules within the `urllib` package to make RESTful requests. The `urllib.parse` module helps us create proper query strings and request bodies. The `urllib.request` module actually makes the Internet connection and gathers the response data. We also used the `json` module because the requests and replies are Python objects in JSON notation.

The request body starts as a dictionary named `request`. We set three of the variables that are used for package search requests. The query is the package subject area; the `start` and `rows` parameters are used to paginate the responses. Waiting for 6,000 responses can take a fairly long time: it's considered unacceptable for an interactive website. Requesting batches of rows using the `start` and `rows` is how we cut down on the time required to respond.

We do a three-step dance to prepare data as part of a RESTful request:

1. Dump the request into JSON notation using the `json` module.

2. Add quote characters so that the JSON will not confuse the HTTP `request` protocol. An HTTP request has a simple syntax and some characters would cause problems if they were part of the request string. For example, an out-of-place space character can make the HTTP request invalid. The `urllib.parse.quote()` function will replace a space with the sequence %20, for example. API servers will unquote the data.

3. Encode the string using UTF-8 encoding rules to create a `bytes` object. All web traffic works in bytes. As a general rule, many (but not all) websites expect the bytes to be a UTF-8 encoding of a string. In some cases, we might have to use ASCII or US-ASCII encoding. UTF-8 is a way to encode the entire domain of Unicode characters. The ASCII (or US-ASCII) encodings use a small subset of characters.

Following the Social Network

We can then open the given URL, allowing us to read the response. There are several parts to the response to a RESTful API request. The HTTP protocol specifies a status, some headers, and a potential body. The HTTP status has a numeric code and a string of text. We're interested in successful requests, which have a numeric code of 200; the text is often the string `"OK"`. We're not interested in the headers — we simply ignored them.

There are a number of commonly used status codes. The general principle is that codes starting with 2 indicate success. Codes starting with 1 are intermediate status, and aren't common in HTTP processing. Codes starting with 3 mean that something more needs to be done to get a useful response. Codes starting with 4 mean that the request is invalid in some way. Codes starting with 5 indicate that the API server is having a problem.

We're very interested in the body of a successful request. To process the body, we do another three-part dance:

1. Read the bytes from the body.
2. Decode the bytes to create a Python string. We follow the general rule of expecting that the bytes are encoded via UTF-8. It's possible that some servers will use ASCII or US-ASCII for their encoding.
3. Use the JSON module to parse the JSON data and create a proper Python object that we can work with. The Python object created will often be a dictionary. Some APIs may respond with a list. In this case, the response is defined as a dictionary with four standard keys.

Once we have the final dictionary object, we can look inside to see the details of the response. The CKAN definitions say that there will be three keys in the dictionary:

- `help`: This will provide more information on the request being made.
- `success`: This will be `True` or `False`.
- `result`: When success is `True`, this will have the expected results. This is the data we wanted; we refer to it as `response_dict['result']` in the function shown previously.
- `Error`: when success is `False`, this will have details of the error.

The general outline of processing shown above is universally true of all requests made to a site using CKAN. We'll create a request object and send the request. We examine the response in two ways: the general HTTP status must be successful and the detailed status inside the response document must also indicate success.

The final part of the processing is unique to the `package_search` request. The response to this request is a dictionary with the requested packages. We only show two parts of this dictionary:

- `response_dict['result']['count']`: This is the overall count of packages that match the search request. We can use this to step through a sequence of page requests. Alternatively, we can make a huge request for everything.

- `response_dict['result']['results']`: This will be a list of individual data packages. There's a wealth of detail describing each package. We haven't shown the details, and we'll leave studying the details to each field agent.

Note that `data.gov` doesn't keep the data itself; they only keep metadata about the package of data. Each individual package will have its own URL that can then be used to access the data. This will, of course, involve additional RESTful API requests to get the data. However, if the data is offered by a site that doesn't use CKAN, then the details of the request and response will not match the CKAN protocol shown here.

The core steps of RESTful API processing as generally very consistent. CKAN illustrates general best practices in using JSON and responding with a standardized dictionary that contains the response as well as more detailed status.

Who's doing the talking?

We'll use the `TwitterAPI` module to gather information about people by using the Twitter social network. This is not necessarily the "best" social network. It's widely-used and has a good API. Other social networking software is also important, and worthy of study. We have to begin somewhere, and Twitter seems to have a fairly low barrier to entry.

In *Chapter 1, New Missions, New Tools*, we downloaded the Twitter API. For information on how to use this package, visit `http://pythonhosted.org/TwitterAPI/`.

The first step to using Twitter is to have a Twitter account. This is easy and free. Agents who don't have a Twitter account can sign up at `http://www.twitter.com`. Once signed up, agents might want to follow the Twitter feed of PacktPub (`https://twitter.com/PacktPub`) to see how Twitter works.

An agent will need to provide a mobile phone number to Twitter to create applications. The information is available here: `https://support.twitter.com/articles/110250-adding-your-mobile-number-to-your-account-via-web`.

Following the Social Network

We need to click on our personal icon in the upper-right corner of the page to get a drop-down menu of choices, one of which is **settings**. On the settings page, there's a long list of specific settings down the left-hand side. The mobile tab is where we enter a phone number. The Twitter platform will send a text message to the given phone number. When we enter the code from that text message, we have provided some small bit of assurance that we're a real human being, not some automated bot trying to abuse the Twitter platform.

In order to use the APIs, we need to sign in to Twitter and generate `oAuth` keys. We'll focus on `oAuth2`, sometimes called application authentication. This gives us read-only access to Twitter. Until we're tasked with counter-intelligence, we won't need to post information. We want to focus on gathering and analyzing information.

We'll wind up at this page: `https://apps.twitter.com/app/new`. Here's what it looks like:

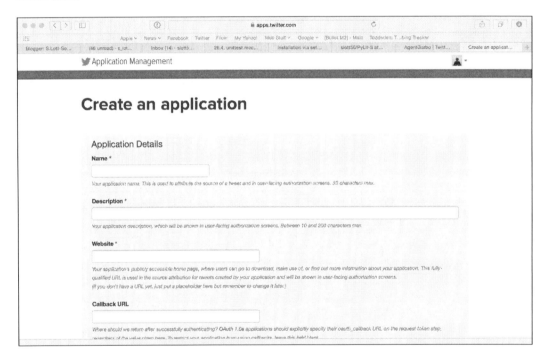

We need to provide three pieces of information:

- **Application name**: This must be short (32 characters at most). We're doing analysis of relationships among people, so we need to pick some name that summarizes this. A clever pun or tricky misspelling is not necessary at this time. An agent code name might work out well.

- **Description**: This can be up to 200 characters summarizing what we're doing.
- **Website**: Ideally, a personal site that might (someday) host an analytical application. Twitter provides this helpful advice: If you don't have a URL yet, just put a placeholder here but remember to change it later. At this point, some agents might want to sign up with the Google Cloud Platform to get a URL they can use to deploy web applications. Visit `https://cloud.google.com/appengine/docs/python/` for more information.

We won't be using the callback feature, so we'll leave the callback URL field empty.

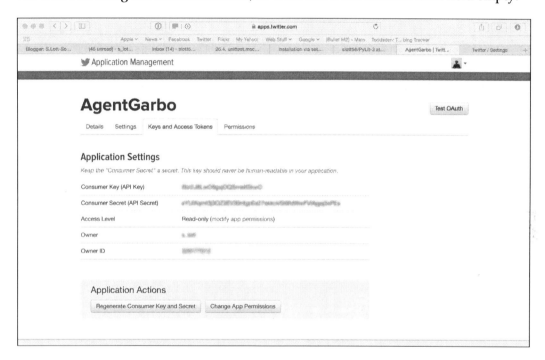

We should read the **Developer Agreement**, particularly part IV on **Ownership** to be sure we see what limitations we need to work under. We'll need to agree to the terms and conditions before we can create our application. Once the application has been created, we'll see a page that includes this information.

We have several things that we'll need to collect from this page. The security tokens that are shown here will become part of each of our Twitter API requests. These tokens are passwords that our application will use to authenticate itself in a general way.

Following the Social Network

For some requests, we'll need the pair of Access Tokens also. This is used to authenticate an individual user to Twitter. Requests which make any changes (for example, posting a new tweet) need both application authentication as well user authentication.

Starting with someone we know

Let's start exploring the social media space by getting some profile information about ourself. We need to have a Twitter account in order to access the social network. What can other users see about us?

When we look at the Twitter API documentation, we start here: `https://dev.twitter.com/overview/documentation`. This includes the REST APIs as well as the streaming APIs. We won't dwell on the streaming data feeds because they involve downloads from Twitter to our computer. We can do this on a personal computer, but it works out better with a larger server that can be dedicated to acquiring, digesting, and publishing data as it arrives.

The interesting bits, however, are here: `https://dev.twitter.com/rest/public`. This section describes the REST APIs that will allow us to probe more selectively into the "Twitterverse" of data. We're going to exercise this API first: `https://dev.twitter.com/rest/reference/get/users/show`.

The documentation shows the complete URL:

```
https://api.twitter.com/1.1/users/show.json
```

This is the complete path to a resource. If we're going to be writing our own processing using `urllib.request`, this is some of the essential information required to build a valid request. Since we're going to be leveraging the `TwitterAPI` module, we don't need to use all of the available details. In fact, we only need the name of the API: `users/show`. This is an abbreviated version of the path to the resource.

The path isn't the entire thing we need to send. We'll also need to send a query string. The default kind of request uses the HTTP GET method, and the data attached to a GET request is often shown after a `?` symbol in the URL.

We also need the consumer key and consumer secret that were issued to us when we signed up. The whole call to Twitter looks like this:

```
from TwitterAPI import TwitterAPI
consumer_key = 'from your application settings page'
consumer_secret = 'also from your application settings'
api = TwitterAPI(consumer_key,
```

[74]

```
                    consumer_secret,
                    auth_type='oAuth2')

response= api.request( 'users/show', {'screen_name':'PacktPub'} )
print( "status", response.status_code )
print( "headers", response.headers )
```

We imported the `TwitterAPI` class from the `TwitterAPI` module. We set two variables with the consumer key and consumer secret information from the application information page. Each agent will need to paste in their own unique consumer key and consumer secret. We're using application-level security, called `oAuth2`; this gives us read-only access.

We create an object, `api`, which contains all of the security overheads. Once we have this object, we can make repeated requests without having to rebuild it.

The `users/show` request requires parameters to clarify which user and whether or not we want the "entities" associated with this account. For information on the entities, visit `https://dev.twitter.com/overview/api/entities`. Entities are hashtags, media, URLs, and user mentions. These are the important details that connect the social network. We're very interested in this.

We printed the status code (usually 200) and the batch of headers. Generally, the headers aren't too interesting, since they're largely technical details. One interesting detail is this header:

```
'x-rate-limit-remaining': '177'
```

This shows us how many requests we can make in a given 15-minute interval. This is shows us how Twitter assures that its servers are responsive. When the limit remaining reaches zero, we're cut off.

The most interesting part of the response, however, is the JSON payload that was downloaded.

Here's a handy way to print that payload:

```
import json
print( json.dumps(response.json(), indent=2) )
```

The value of `response.json()` is the Python object that had been encoded into JSON notation by the Twitter server. This is often a dictionary, but it can also be a list. We used the `json` module to create a nicely-formatted dump by rebuilding the JSON object from the Python object.

Following the Social Network

This does double the effort by creating a Python object from JSON and then recreating some JSON. It also introduces a tiny bit of variability because the Python object will use a default dictionary that does not guarantee the order of the keys. It's much easier to read, and it is worth the effort to make debugging easier.

The output is immense. It starts like this:

```
{
  "contributors_enabled": false,
  "is_translation_enabled": false,
  "favourites_count": 494,
  "profile_link_color": "0084B4",
  "profile_sidebar_fill_color": "CC9933",
  "profile_background_color": "FFA200",
  "has_extended_profile": false,
  "profile_background_image_url_https": "https://pbs.twimg.com/
profile_background_images/498821312354058242/-H6BGz56.png",
  "profile_background_image_url": "http://pbs.twimg.com/profile_
background_images/498821312354058242/-H6BGz56.png",
  "statuses_count": 9651,
  "profile_image_url_https": "https://pbs.twimg.com/profile_
images/622000526033592320/oHzUsSbm_normal.png",
  "profile_location": null,
  "utc_offset": 3600,
  "name": "Packt Publishing",
  "url": "http://t.co/vEPCgOu235",
```

It continues on for many more lines of code. There's a lot of technical details that Twitter makes available.

Finding our followers

The really important features of a social network are the connections among the people. Twitter exposes this with two sets of relationships: who follows a user and who a user is following; the latter group are called friends.

Relationships are directional. If A has a friend B, then A is usually notified when B posts something (unless B is muted). This is revealed from A's friend list. In addition, we will also see A placed in B's followers list; which is a redundant description of the relationship. If B has a friend A, then the relationship is mutual. We line from A to B or B to A has a start viewpoint and an end viewpoint.

Connections among a larger group can, of course, be considerably more complex.

There are (at most) $\dfrac{n \times (n-1)}{2}$ possible connections among n people. This is `sum(range(n))`. The proof is interesting, but we'll leave it to each agent to work out the details of why this has to be true.

Who follows us? We'll need to make a query for the `followers/list` resource. This query is rather complex because there could be multiple pages of responses. Imagine someone who has millions of followers: a single response listing all the followers would be huge. Twitter sends back results in batches using fields called "cursors" to allow paging forward (and backward) through the results. Visit `https://dev.twitter.com/overview/api/cursoring` for more information on how this works.

We'll need to take a more intentional approach to working with cursors. We need to address an issue sometimes called the "loop and a half" problem. Visit `https://www.cs.duke.edu/~ola/patterns/plopd/loops.html#loop-and-a-half` for a brief summary.

This is a common design concern. From one point of view, we want to exit in the middle of the indented code in a `while` statement: we're forced to use an `if...break` statement, which makes the condition on the `while` statement itself moot. From another point of view, we have asymmetric processing around the cursor: either the first or last response has to be handled outside the `while` statement. While many agents are comfortable with the `break` statement, HQ prefers to avoid it if possible: they recommend the status variable pattern shown below.

Our `list_followers_by_screen_name()` function will accept a screen name and will print all of the followers. These are the direct followers: people who will be notified of a tweet. Beyond them is a second tier of followers who will see retweets. This second tier can be surprisingly large.

We'll break this function into two parts. In the first part, we'll define a nested function to display useful information from the response object:

```python
def list_followers_by_screen_name(screen_name):
    counter= 0
    def show_user_list( response ):
        nonlocal counter
        for u in response['users']:
            print( u['name'], u['screen_name'], u['friends_count'] )
            counter += 1
```

Following the Social Network

This inner `show_user_list()` function steps through the response object, showing all of the items associated with the `'users'` key. This value is a list of objects that show detailed information about each Twitter user in the response. Since this is inside a function that fetches followers, each user displayed will be a follower of some central user.

We used the `nonlocal` statement so that we can increment the counter variable that's part of the parent function. The `nonlocal` statement is rarely needed; without it, however, there's no other good way to do this simple thing. The alternatives either involve global variables or error-prone complications.

For each user, we're just printing a few things. The friends count shows us how large the social circle becomes when we include friends of our followers.

We don't technically need a nested function for this. However, it seems slightly simpler to disentangle the display portions from the request portions of the overall function. We'll often tweak the display without needing to disturb the larger context of request and response handling.

The second part of the `list_followers_by_screen_name()` function does the request processing:

```
api = TwitterAPI(consumer_key,
                 consumer_secret,
                 auth_type='oAuth2')
cursor= -1
while cursor != 0:
    response= api.request( 'followers/list',
        {'screen_name':screen_name, 'cursor':cursor} )
    assert response.status_code == 200, "Request failed: {text}\
n{headers}".format_map(vars(response))
    body= response.json()
    show_user_list(body)
    cursor= body['next_cursor']
print( "Total {counter}".format_map(vars) )
```

We build the `TwitterAPI` object using the required application keys. We can then use this object to make multiple requests. In a larger or more complex application, we'll often build just one of these during initialization, and use it throughout the application's processing.

We initialized a status variable, `cursor`, to the starting value of `-1`. This tells the Twitter application that this is our first request and we want to start at the beginning of the list of followers.

Chapter 3

The actual request uses the resource path, `'followers/list'`, and two parameter values: the screen name of the user we're asking about and the cursor value used to step through the result set. Initially, the `cursor` value is `-1`, but this will change with each request.

We used an assert statement to show that our request has a `status_code` value of 200. If the value is not 200, this will raise an `AssertionError`. We could use an `if...raise` statement for this. The problem with the `assert` statement is that it's terribly long. The most common error will be running afoul of the rate limiting rules in Twitter. An agent to tries to gather too much data too quickly will find themselves cutoff temporarily.

We decoded the body object from its JSON representation and provided this object to our nested function, `show_user_list()`. This will display information about the followers. It will also count the total number of followers.

We then extracted the value of `body['next_cursor']` from the response object. If this is 0, there is no more data. If this is non-zero, we must provide it in our request so that we get the next batch of followers. We update the `cursor` variable so that our while statement has an invariant condition: a non-zero cursor value means we can make a valid request.

How many second-tier followers do we see in the results?

We'll need to tweak this program to do more than simply count followers. We'll need some additional variables, and we'll need to update the nonlocal statement. This is your mission: count up the second-tier followers.

What do they seem to be talking about?

Finding the social network is only the first step. We want to examine the conversation, also. We'll look at two aspects of this conversion: words and pictures. Our first background mission in this section was to be sure we had Pillow working properly. This will also help us download pictures.

Words are somewhat simpler. Interestingly, the tweet content isn't obvious in the Twitter API definitions. It turns out that "status" is what we're looking for. The resource called `statuses/user_timeline` has the tweets made by a given user.

Each status or tweet is packaged with a collection of entities. These are the URL references, media attachments, @ user_mentions, # hashtags, and $ symbols. The entities are separated from the body of the tweet, which greatly simplifies our analysis.

[79]

Following the Social Network

Here's a function to get the last 20 tweets from a user:

```python
def tweets_by_screen_name(screen_name):
    api = TwitterAPI(consumer_key,
                    consumer_secret,
                    auth_type='oAuth2')
    response= api.request( 'statuses/user_timeline',
                            {'screen_name':screen_name, 'count':20}
    )
    for item in response.json():
        text= item['text']
        entities= item['entities']
        # entities include $symbols, @user_mentions, #hashtags, urls,
    media
        sym_list = [s['text'] for s in entities['symbols']]
        user_list = [u['screen_name'] for u in entities['user_
    mentions']]
        hash_list = [h['text'] for h in entities['hashtags']]
        url_list = [u['expanded_url'] for u in entities['urls']]
        if 'media' in entities:
            media_list = [m['media_url'] for m in entities['media']]
        else:
            media_list = []
        print( item['text'], "$", sym_list, "@", user_list,
            "#", hash_list, url_list, media_list )
```

As with the previous examples, we build an instance of `TwitterAPI` using our two keys. We used this object to request the `statuses/user_timeline` resource for a particular screen name. We limited this to the last 20 tweets to keep the response small and focused.

The response object will be a list of individual status tweets. We can iterate through that object, processing each individual item separately. The value of `item['text']` is the actual tweet. But there's a great deal of additional information about the tweet. We decomposed the various entities associated with a tweet to show some of the details available.

The value of `item['entities']` will be a dictionary with a number of keys, including `'symbols'`, `'user_mentions'`, `'hashtags'`, `'urls'`, and (optionally) `'media'`. Each one of these various kinds of entities has a number of attributes, including the text value that was part of the original tweet and the indices that show the character position occupied by the entity. Some entity types are pure text, with no additional details. Other entity types (such as URLs and media) have considerable additional detail. We'll look at the media separately.

[80]

We used a list comprehension to create a list of values from each type of entity. Each comprehension is similar to this:

```
[s['text'] for s in entities['symbols']]
```

This will iterate through the sequence of values found in entities['symbols']. Each of those objects is a tiny dictionary, which is assigned to the s variable inside the for expression. The values of s['text'] become the resulting list.

Here's the thing which is printed from this:

```
What does the #appdev industry look like today? Find out with our
#SkillUp report! http://t.co/ocxVJQBbiW http://t.co/nKkntoDWbs $ [] @
[] # ['appdev', 'SkillUp'] ['http://bit.ly/PacktDailyOffer'] ['http://
twitter.com/PacktPub/status/626678626734333956/photo/1']
```

You can see the text of the tweet first. There are no $ symbols, nor any specific @ user mentions. There are two # hashtags: appdev and SkillUp. There's a URL in the tweet as well as a chunk of media associated with the tweet. We can pursue the URL's to download additional content related to this tweet.

This leads us to several additional topics: we can download the media objects to see the images. As we noted in the first background briefing, we need to use Pillow to confirm that these files are valid. We can open the referenced URL and use BeautifulSoup to extract the text from the page to get detailed additional content.

We can also use more advanced Twitter search functions to examine hashtags, user mentions, followers, and friends. One interesting bit of intelligence gathering is to rank followers and friends based on their rate of retweeting. We can locate influencers this way by tracking popular retweeted content back to its source.

What are they posting?

To gather images being posted, we'll modify our query that retrieves tweets. We'll get the media URL from the tweet, use urllib.request to get the image file, and use Pillow to confirm that it's a valid image and create a thumbnail of the image. While there are a lot of steps, each of them is something we've already seen.

We'll break this function into two parts: the Twitter part and the image processing part. Here's the first part, making the essential Twitter request:

```
import urllib.request
import urllib.parse
from PIL import Image
import io
```

Following the Social Network

```python
def tweet_images_by_screen_name(screen_name):
    api = TwitterAPI(consumer_key,
                     consumer_secret,
                     auth_type='oAuth2')
    response= api.request( 'statuses/user_timeline',
                           {'screen_name':screen_name, 'count':30}
    )
    for item in response.json():
        text= item['text']
        entities= item['entities']
        if 'media' in entities:
            media_list = entities['media']
        else:
            media_list = []
        print( item['text'], item['entities'].keys(), media_list )
```

The four imports are entirely focused on extracting the image file. We'll look at those next.

As with other examples, we created the essential `TwitterAPI` object. We make a request for the `statuses/user_timeline` resource, providing the screen name of someone whose images we want to examine. For each tweet, we extract the text and the entities. From the entities, we extract the list of media items, if the `'media'` key is present in the entities dictionary. We can print the tweet and the details of the media.

The output will include lines like this:

```
Use #Pentaho? Grab our free eBook and handle all kinds of data
manipulation! http://t.co/ocxVJQBbiW http://t.co/Wsu93Xpizo dict_
keys(['urls', 'user_mentions', 'media', 'hashtags', 'symbols'])
[{'type': 'photo', 'id': 626316242257776640, 'url': 'http://t.co/
Wsu93Xpizo', 'indices': [100, 122], 'display_url': 'pic.twitter.com/
Wsu93Xpizo', 'id_str': '626316242257776640', 'expanded_url': 'http://
twitter.com/PacktPub/status/626316242329034752/photo/1', 'media_url_
https': 'https://pbs.twimg.com/media/CLEfTdDVEAAHw1i.png', 'media_
url': 'http://pbs.twimg.com/media/CLEfTdDVEAAHw1i.png', 'sizes':
{'large': {'w': 590, 'h': 295, 'resize': 'fit'}, 'thumb': {'w': 150,
'h': 150, 'resize': 'crop'}, 'small': {'w': 340, 'h': 170, 'resize':
'fit'}, 'medium': {'w': 590, 'h': 295, 'resize': 'fit'}}}]
```

Notice that Twitter provides size information for large, medium, and small, versions of the image using information like `'resize': 'fit'`. This can be useful for scaling the image and maintaining the shape. It also provides `'thumb': {'w': 150, 'h': 150, 'resize': 'crop'}`. This seems to be advice on cropping the image down to a smaller size; we don't think this is as useful as the other sizing information.

[82]

Here's the second part, processing each image in the entities list associated with a tweet:

```
for media_item in media_list:
    url_text = media_item['media_url']
    parsed_name= urllib.parse.urlparse(url_text)
    filename= parsed_name.path.split('/')[-1]
    with urllib.request.urlopen(url_text) as image_file:
        data = image_file.read()
    temp_file = io.BytesIO(data)
    im = Image.open(temp_file)
    im.show()
    #im.save(filename)
```

We saved the value of the `'media_url'` in the `url_text` variable. We then used the `urllib.parse.urlparse()` function to parse this URL so that we can decompose the full URL and get a filename. The result of parsing is a `namedtuple` with the various elements of a URL, which we assigned to the `parsed_name` variable. From this variable, we used the `parsed_name.path` attribute, which ends with a filename.

For example, `http://pbs.twimg.com/media/CLEfTdDVEAAHw1i.png` has a path `media/CLEfTdDVEAAHw1i.png`. When we split the path on / characters, the final entry is the filename, `CLEfTdDVEAAHw1i.png`.

We use `urllib.request.urlopen()` to open the URL. We do this inside a `with` statement so that it acts as a context manager and releases any network resources at the end of the overall `with` statement. We read the data without actually saving a local file on our computer. We need to confirm that the image is valid.

We created an `io.BytesIO` object from the bytes read from the file. This is a file-like object that `PIL.Image` can use instead of an actual file on a local computer. If the image can be opened, it's a valid file. Now, we can do things like show it, save it to our local computer, or create a thumbnail version of the image.

Deep Under Cover – NLTK and language analysis

As we study Twitter more and more, we see that they've made an effort to expose numerous details of the social network. They've parsed the Tweet to extract hashtags and user mentions, they've carefully organized the media. This makes a great deal of analysis quite simple.

Following the Social Network

On the other hand, some parts of the analysis are still quite difficult. The actual topic of a Twitter conversion is just a string of characters. It's essentially opaque until a person reads the characters to understand the words and the meaning behind the words.

Understanding natural-language text is a difficult problem. We often assign it to human analysts. If we can dump the related tweets into a single easy-to-read document, then a person can scan it, summarize, and decide if this is actionable intelligence or just background noise.

One of the truly great counter-intelligence missions is Operation Mincemeat. There are many books that describe this operation. What's import about this is that the Allies provided enough related information to make the false intelligence data appear true. The Mincemeat data had the feel of truth to enough of the Axis intelligence service, that it was trusted.

It's often difficult to judge between truth and clever fiction. That's an inherently human job. What we can automate, however, is the collection and summarization of data to support that judgment.

Artificial languages like JSON or Python have rigid, inflexible rules for grammar and syntax. Natural languages like English don't have any actual rules. What we have are conventions that many people know. Native speakers learn a language from parents, care-givers, neighbors, teachers, media, vendors, customers, and so on. While teachers can try to impose grammar rules, they're not fixed, and they're rarely even required. Book publishers—in an effort to reach the widest-possible audience—stick assiduously to widely-accepted grammar rules.

Children don't know the grammar rules, make outrageous mistakes, and are still understood. Indeed, we often chuckle at children who "goed to the store with mommy." We know they went to the store even though they used a non-word to express themselves. We can't use the `primt()` function in Python. We get a syntax error and that's it; the compiler doesn't chuckle politely and suggest we meant `print()`. This is a profound difference between people's ability to understand and software tools that parse text.

As human members of social networks, we follow only the grammar rules that apply within a given social context. In some contexts, the term "7331 h4x0r" is perfectly meaningful. To other people, the jumble of symbols looks like a technical glitch. This applies across languages, as well as applying across cultures that use a common language. Compare British English, Australian English, and American English. A common-seeming word like jumper can have a wide variety of meanings.

While the problem is hugely complex, there are tools we can apply. The premier tool for natural language processing is the Python NLTK. For many kinds of analysis, this tool is central and essential. Some people learn Python only so that they can use NLTK for analysis of text.

NLTK and natural language analysis is too complex to address here. Agents are encouraged to study material like the *Python 3 Text Processing with NLTK 3 Cookbook* by author *Jacob Perkins*:

```
https://www.packtpub.com/application-development/python-3-text-
processing-nltk-3-cookbook
```

It's difficult to provide more than a few ideas here. We'll suggest that there are two common strategies that can help with natural language analysis:

- Word Stemming
- Stop Words

Word stemming refers to stripping away prefixes and suffixes to get to the stem of a word. We know that "goes", "went", and "going" are all related to the verb "to go" in spite of the problem that "went" is spelled completely differently. By stemming words, we can strip away features that aren't as helpful in an effort to look for the real meaning.

Stop words are connectives that don't materially impact the subject of the text. Words like "the" and "an" are called stop words because we don't need to process them. The exact list of stop words relevant to a particular problem domain requires careful research.

Interested agents will need to pursue this on their own. It's beyond the scope of these missions.

Summary

We discussed the basics of automated analysis of the social network. We looked at one particular social network: the people who use Twitter to exchange messages. This is about 316 million active users, exchanging about 500 million messages a month. We saw how to find information about specific people, about the list of friends a person follows, and the tweets a person makes.

We also discussed how to download additional media from social networking sites. We used PIL to confirm that an image is saved to work with. We also used PIL to create thumbnails of images. We can do a great deal of processing to gather and analyze data that people readily publish about themselves.

Following the Social Network

In the next chapter, we'll look at another source of data that's often difficult to work with. The ubiquitous PDF file format is difficult to process without specialized tools. The file is designed to allow consistent display and printing of documents. It's not, however, too helpful for analysis of content. We'll need to leverage several tools to crack open the contents of a PDF file.

4
Dredging up History

Parse PDF files to locate data that's otherwise nearly inaccessible. The web is full of PDF files, many of which contain valuable intelligence. The problem is extracting this intelligence in a form where we can analyze it. Some PDF text can be extracted with sophisticated parsers. At other times, we have to resort to **Optical Character Recognition (OCR)** because the PDF is actually an image created with a scanner. How can we leverage information that's buried in PDFs?

In some cases, we can use a **save as text** option to try and expose the PDF content. We then replace a PDF parsing problem with a plain-text parsing problem. While PDFs can seem dauntingly complex, the presence of exact page coordinates can actually simplify our efforts at gleaning information.

Also, some PDFs have fill-in-the-blanks features. If we have one of these, we'll be parsing the annotations within the PDF. This is similar to parsing the text of the PDF.

The most important consideration here is that a PDF is focused on printing and display. It's not designed to be useful for analysis. In order to overcome this limitation, we'll need to have a powerful toolkit available. The primary tool is Python extended with the PDFMiner3k module.

The other tools in this toolkit are our personal collection of functions and classes that we can use to extract meaningful content from PDFs. There's no single, universal solution to this problem. Different documents will require different kinds of tweaks and adjustments to handle the document's unique features. We'll show some of the functions that serve as a starting point in building this toolkit. As agents pursue more and more information, they will inevitably build up their own toolkits of unique classes and functions.

Dredging up History

This section will cover the following topics:

- We'll start with a background briefing on PDF documents.

- We'll also review the Python techniques of generator functions that can yield sequential pieces of a complex document. This will speed up processing by allowing us to focus on meaningful content and avoid some of the overheads that are part of PDFs.

- We'll also look at how Python context managers and the `with` statement can fit nicely with picking apart the content in a PDF.

- We'll pull these threads together to create a resource manager that helps us filter and extract text from PDFs.

- Once we have the raw text, we can use layout information to understand how tables are represented so that we can extract meaningful tabular data.

- We'll tweak the layout parameters to help PDFMiner assemble meaningful blocks of text from complex tabular layouts.

- Finally, we'll emit useful CSV-format data for further analysis.

Once we get the real underlying data, we can apply techniques we saw in *Chapter 2, Tracks, Trails, and Logs*, to the raw data.

Background briefing–Portable Document Format

The PDF file format dates from 1991. Here's a quote from Adobe's website about the format: *it can capture documents from any application, send electronic versions of these documents anywhere, and view and print these documents on any machines.* The emphasis is clearly on view and print. What about analysis?

There's an ISO standard that applies to PDF documents, assuring us that no single vendor has a lock on the technology. The standard has a focus on specific technical design, user interface or implementation or operational details of rendering. The presence of a standard doesn't make the document file any more readable or useful as a long-term information archive.

What's the big problem?

Chapter 4

The Wikipedia page summarizes three technologies that are part of a PDF document:

- A subset of the PostScript page description programming language, for generating the page layout and graphics
- Font management within the document
- A document storage structure, including compression, to create a single file

Of these, it's the page layout that causes the most problems.

The PostScript language describes the look of a page of text. It doesn't require that the text on that page is provided in any coherent order. This is different from HTML or XML, where tags can be removed from the HTML source and a sensible plain text document can be recovered.

In PostScript, text is commingled with page layout commands in such a way that the underlying sequence of characters, words, sentences and paragraphs can be lost. Pragmatically, complete obfuscation of a page is rare. Many documents occupy a middle ground where the content is difficult to parse. One common quirk is out-of-place headline text; we have to use the coordinates on the page to deduce where it belongs in the text.

PDF can be abused too. In the most extreme cases, people will print some content, scan the pages, and build a PDF around the scanned images. This kind of document will display and print nicely. But it defies simple analysis. More complex OCR is required to deal with this. This is beyond our scope, since the algorithms can be very complex.

Here's a typical document that contains mountains of useful data. However, it's hard to access because it's locked up in a PDF (`http://bhpr.hrsa.gov/ healthworkforce/data/compendiumfederaldatasources.pdf`). The title is the *Compendium of Federal Data Sources to Support Health Workforce Analysis April 2013*.

Agents interested in industrial espionage—particularly about the workforce—would need to understand the various sources in this document.

Some agents agree that governments (and industry) use PDFs entirely to provide data in a "see-but-don't-touch" mode. We can only leverage the data through expensive, error-prone, manual operations. We can't easily reach out and touch the data digitally to do deeper analysis.

[89]

Dredging up History

Extracting PDF content

In *Chapter 1, New Missions – New Tools*, we installed PDF Miner 3K to parse PDF files. It's time to see how this tool works. Here's the link to the documentation for this package: `http://www.unixuser.org/~euske/python/pdfminer/index.html`. This link is not obvious from the PyPI page, or from the BitBucket site that contains the software. An agent who scans the `docs/index.html` will see this reference.

In order to see how we use this package, visit `http://www.unixuser.org/~euske/python/pdfminer/programming.html`. This has an important diagram that shows how the various classes interact to represent the complex internal details of a PDF document. For some helpful insight, visit `http://denis.papathanasiou.org/posts/2010.08.04.post.html`.

A PDF document is a sequence of physical pages. Each page has boxes of text (in addition to images and line graphics). Each textbox contains lines of text and each line contains the individual characters. Each of these layers has positioning information. For the most part, the textbox positions are the most interesting, and we can use those to disentangle complex documents. Our focus is on the central relationships of document, page, and textbox within the page.

There may be additional information like forms that can be filled in, or thumbnails that provide an outline of the document. This information can also be extracted from the PDF. Seeing the outline can be handy, so we'll start with that.

In order to work with PDF Miner, we'll create a parsing class. We'll use a class definition for this because some elements of the parsing process are a bit too complex for separate functions. Because of the complex entanglements of **PDFParser**, **PDFDocument**, **PDFResourceManager**, and **PDFPageInterpreter**, we'll want to use a context manager to be sure that all of the resources are released when we're done working with a given file.

Using generator expressions

Before we can dig into the nuances of PDFs, we'll need to address a Python programming feature that the PDFMiner relies on: the generator function. A generator function behaves in some ways like a sequence collection. The important difference is that a sequence collection is created eagerly, where a generator function is lazy.

- **Eager**: All the items in collection are created and saved in memory.
- **Lazy**: The items in the collection aren't created until they demanded by a `for` loop or a function that created a collection like `list()`, `tuple()`, `set()`, or `dict()`.

Chapter 4

The simplest kind of generator is a generator expression. We provide three pieces of information in a syntax that looks much like a `for` statement:

(*expression* `for` *variable* `in` *source*)

The overall expression has an expression which is evaluated with a variable assigned each value from some source. We might use a **range()** object as a source. We might use an existing list, tuple, set, or dict, also. We can even use a file as a source of lines.

Here's an example:

```
>>> gen= (2*i+1 for i in range(10))
>>> gen
<generator object <genexpr> at 0x1007a1318>
```

The generator expression didn't create anything interesting. The value of the `gen` variable is the generator. The output is an obscure note that it's a generator object based on a `<genexpr>`. Since the object is lazy, it won't produce anything until required.

Here's an example of building a list object from a generator:

```
>>> list(gen)
[1, 3, 5, 7, 9, 11, 13, 15, 17, 19]
```

When we applied the `list()` function to the generator expression, the values were produced by the generator and consumed by the `list()` function to create a resulting list object.

We can also consume the items manually with a `for` statement. It would look like this:

```
>>> gen2 = (2*i+1 for i in range(10))
>>> s = 0
>>> for x in gen2:
...       print(x)
...       s += x
1
3
5
etc.
```

We created a second generator, `gen2`, which is identical to `gen`. We used a `for` statement to consume items from the generator. In this case, we produced output and we also computed the sum of the various items in the list.

It's important to note that generators can only produce their data items once. If we try to use the `gen` or `gen2` generators for anything else, we'll find that they won't produce any more values:

```
>>> list(gen)
[]
>>> list(gen2)
[]
```

We have to bear this rule in mind when working the generator expressions in the PDFMiner3k package.

> Generator expression can be consumed only once.

The lazy nature of generators makes them ideal for dealing with large, complex PDF documents in a pure Python application. A program written in C or C++ can process PDFs very quickly. A library that leverages special PDF-parsing libraries can be very fast. PDFMiner3k doesn't have these speedups, so it relies on Python generators to do as little work as it possibly can.

Writing generator functions

A generator function looks a lot like a simple function with one important change. A generator function includes a `yield` statement. Each time the `yield` statement is executed, another value is produced. This can be consumed by a `list()` function or a `for` loop.

A generator function looks like this:

```
def gen_function(start):
    c = start
    for i in range(10):
        yield c
        if c%2 == 0:
            c= c//2
        else:
            c= 3*c+1
```

Chapter 4

This function will yield 10 values based on a fairly complex calculation that is based on the starting value. This uses the half or triple plus one (HOTPO) rule to compute each subsequent value. Here's how we can use this generator function:

```
>>> gen_function(13) # doctest: +ELLIPSIS
<generator object gen_function at ...>
>>> list(gen_function(13))
[13, 40, 20, 10, 5, 16, 8, 4, 2, 1]
```

We try to apply the function to an argument and all we get is a generator object. When we use a function like `list()`, the lazy generator expression is forced to produce all of its values. The `list()` function consumes the values and creates a list object.

An interesting exercise is to replace the `for` statement with `while c != 1`. Will the loop always yield a finite sequence of values?

We'll use these concepts of generator expression and generator function to examine the contents of a PDF file. Perhaps the single more important concept is that generators are lazy and yield their values one time only. After the values have been consumed, the generator appears to be empty.

Filtering bad data

One of the important uses for generator expressions and generator functions is filtering bad data. We can use either of these—as well as third technique—to reject bad data or pass good data.

The generator expression has an additional clause available:

(*expression* for *variable* in *source* if *condition*)

This will apply the `if` condition to each value in the source. If the condition is true, the internal expression is the value that's kept. If the condition is false, the value is ignored.

For example, we might have something like this:

```
>>> fb = (n for n in range(10) if n % 3 == 0 or n % 5 == 0)
>>> sum(fb)
23
```

We've started with a source that's a `range()` object. We'll assign each value to the variable n. If the value of n is a multiple of three or a multiple of five, the value that's kept is simply n. If the value of n is neither a multiple of three nor a multiple of five, the value is ignored.

Dredging up History

The resulting values can be processed by a function that can consume generator expressions. We could use `list()` or `tuple()` to keep the individual values. Instead, we reduced the sequence to a single value.

We can add an `if` statement to a generator function, too. This shouldn't be too surprising.

The third way we can filter is by using a separate function available in Python: the `filter()` function. This requires two things: a function that decides which values to pass and which to reject, and an iterable sequence of values. The `filter()` function is a generator: it's lazy and won't produce answers unless we demand them. Here's how we can use `filter()` as if it was a generator expression:

```
>>> fb2 = filter(lambda n: n%3==0 or n%5==0, range(10))
>>> sum(fb2)
23
```

We've written a very small function to evaluate whether or not n is a multiple of three or a multiple of five. The function is so small we didn't even provide a name, just the parameter and the expression we would have placed on a `return` statement. We write tiny one-expression functions using the lambda form: `lambda` *parameters* `:` *expression*. We've provided the source of data, the `range(10)` object. The filter function does the rest: it iterates through the source, applies the given lambda function to each value, and produces the individual values for which the function is true. Values for which the function are false are rejected.

As with a generator expression, the value of `fb2` is the cryptic-looking `<filter object at 0x1023ce9e8>`. We have to consume the values with `list()`, `tuple()`, `sum()`, a `for` statement, or some other function, because it's lazy and not eager. In this example, we consumed the values with the `sum()` function.

As we noted previously, we can only consume the values from the `fb` or `fb2` variables one time. If we try to use these variables again, they won't yield any more values.

We'll switch gears here, and look at a second import Python design pattern. This will help us deal with the complexity of files and parsers for the file content.

Writing a context manager

In addition to generator functions, we'll also need another Python design pattern: the context manager. We'll need to define a context manager so that we can work with the parser, the document, and the open file object. After processing a PDF file, we want to be sure that all of the related objects are properly released from memory.

Chapter 4

A context manager is easily built via a class definition. The object will have three stages in its life:

1. We create a context manager object. The __init__() method handles this.

2. We enter the context. This is what happens when a `with` statement starts execution. The __enter__() method is invoked; the value returned is the object assigned via the "as" clause in a `with` statement. While this is often the context manager itself, it doesn't actually have to be. It could some more useful object that the application will use.

3. We exit the context. This is what happens when we leave the `with` statement. The __exit__() method is invoked. There are two ways to leave a `with` statement: normal exit and an exception-caused exit. Exceptional exits will include parameters with details about the exception. Normal exits will have no additional details.

Here's how a context manager looks in a `with` statement.

```
with ContextManager() ❶ as cm: ❷
    cm.method()
    ❸
next statement after the context
```

We've decorated this to show the life cycle events. Here's the outline of a context manager class definition. We've added the numbers to show how the two fit together.

```
class ContextManager:
    def __init__(self):  ❶
        "Build the context manager."
    def __enter__(self): ❷
        "Enter the context. The return value is assigned via the `as`
clause"
        return self
    def __exit__(self, *exc): ❸
        "Exit the context. Return True to silence the exception."
```

The __init__() method from a context manager is (usually) where we'll open a file or create a network connection or otherwise allocate resources. We'll create the various PDFMiner objects here. A common implementation of the __enter__() method returns the context manager itself as a useful object. Since the initialization handled all the hard work of building the context object, nothing more needs to be done here. The __exit__() method should delete all of the resources allocated by the __init__() method. The default return value of None will allow exceptions to propagate normally after __exit__() has released the resources.

[95]

Writing a PDF parser resource manager

The complexity of PDF documents means that the PDFMiner3k package requires a fairly complex initialization. At a minimum, we need to parse the contents of the PDF file and represent the document that is found within that complex file structure. The initialization will get more complex as we seek to get more detail from the PDF file.

We'll start our software design with a basic context manager. We'll use inheritance to add features as we seek to gather more and more data from the document. We'll show the context manager class definition in two parts. We'll start with the __init__() method:

```python
from pdfminer.pdfparser import PDFParser, PDFDocument
class Miner:
    def __init__(self, filename, password=''):
        self.fp = open(filename, 'rb')
        self.parser = PDFParser(self.fp)
        self.doc = PDFDocument()
        self.parser.set_document(self.doc)
        self.doc.set_parser(self.parser)
        self.doc.initialize(password)
```

This class initialization method creates three closely-related objects: the open file object, the parser which extracts details from the document, and the document object that we can examine to find some of the PDF content. In the later examples, we'll build on this by adding more and more objects that are part of the parsing.

Note that we must call the `initialize()` method of the document even if the document has no password protection. For documents without a password, we should provide a zero-length string object, which is the default value for the password parameter.

In order to be a proper context manager, there are two additional methods we need to define:

```python
    def __enter__(self):
        return self
    def __exit__(self, *args):
        self.fp.close()
        del self.doc._parser
        del self.parser.doc
        self.doc = None
        self.parser = None
```

We defined the minimal __enter__() method that simply returns the `self` instance variable. We defined an __exit__() method that will close the file object and remove references to the document and parser objects. Agents who look closely at the PDFMiner3k implementation will see that there are mutual object references between document and parser; in order to assure that the objects aren't both stuck in memory, we explicitly break the mutual connection.

We can use the `Miner` context manager like this:

```
with Miner(filename) as miner:
    outlines = miner.doc.get_outlines()
    toc = [ (level, title) for (level,title,dest,a,se) in outlines
]
    pprint( toc )
```

This evaluates the `get_outlines()` method of the `PDFDocument` object inside the `Miner` object. This method returns a generator function. The value of `get_outlines()` is not a list: it's a generator which can be used to build a list. The generator will yield five tuples that contain outline information.

When we create the `toc` list using list comprehension, we're forcing the lazy `get_outlines()` method to actually build outline strings from the document. Each outline contains a level number, a title, and a reference to a PDF object. The `a` and `se` attributes of the five tuple always have a value of `None`, so we'll ignore them.

This function will dump the outline information from the document. Not all documents have outlines, so it's possible that this will raise an exception.

The most important part about this is that it shows the basics of how to use parts of PDFMiner3k. We'll build on this to get pages and then get the layout objects within each page.

Extending the resource manager

We'll leverage inheritance to add some additional features to our context manager. Rather than rewrite the entire context manager, or (even worse) copy and paste the code from one context manager to create another, we'll create a new one which extends the previous one. This principle of object-oriented class extension via inheritance allows us to create closely-related families of classes that reuse critical features without introducing errors by copying code.

Dredging up History

Here's the initial portion of the class definition:

```
from pdfminer.pdfinterp import PDFResourceManager, PDFPageInterpreter
from pdfminer.pdfdevice import PDFDevice
class Miner_Page(Miner):
    def __init__(self, filename, password='', **kw):
        super().__init__(filename, password)
        self.resources = PDFResourceManager()
        self.device = self.init_device(self.resources, **kw)
        self.interpreter = PDFPageInterpreter(self.resources, self.
device)
    def init_device(self, resource_manager, **params):
        """Return a generic PDFDevice object without parameter
settings."""
        return PDFDevice(resource_manager)
    def init_device(self, resource_manager, **params):
        """Return a generic PDFDevice object without parameter
settings."""
        return PDFDevice(resource_manager)
```

The `Miner_Page` subclass of `Miner` uses a common Python technique for extending the `__init__()` method to add new features. We've defined the subclass `__init__()` method using the same parameters as the parent class, plus we've added `**kw`. This means that any additional keyword argument values are collected into a single dictionary and assigned to the `kw` parameter. We provide the positional parameters to the superclass. We use the keyword parameters when building a device.

The `super()` function locates this object's superclass, which is the `Miner` class. Using `super().__init__()` is slightly more generic (and easier to understand) than trying to use `Miner.__init__()`; the `super()` function also sets the `self` variable for us. We've passed the positional arguments and keyword parameters to the superclass `__init__()`: this delegates the details of initialization to the `Miner` class.

Once the basics are taken care of, this `Miner_Page` subclass can create the three additional components we need for extract text from PDF files. The `PDFResourceManager` and a `PDFDevice` tools are required to process the PostScript commands that describe a page of text. We put the creation of the device into a separate method, `init_device()`. The `PDFPageInterpreter` tool uses the resource manager and the device to process the PostScript commands.

It turns out that we'll need to change the way a `PDFDevice` instance is created. We've isolated this detail into a separate method; a subclass will override this method and add yet more clever features. For now, we've provided an object which will extract some useful information from PDF page.

Chapter 4

We can see that there are three separate design principles for methods in a class:

- The method is required to support a particular interface. The __enter__()
  and __exit__() methods for interacting with the with statement are
  examples of this.

- The method is helpful for isolating a feature that is subject to change.
  The init_device() is an example of this.

- The method does something we need. We'll look at these kinds of
  methods next.

We'll add one more method to this class so that we can process each page of the
document. This will wrap the PDFDocument get_pages() method so that we can
get the text of the page.

```python
def page_iter(self):
    """Yields a PDFPage for each page in the document."""
    for page in self.doc.get_pages():
        self.interpreter.process_page(page)
        yield page
```

This function applies the interpreter object to each page. The interpreter uses
the resource manager and the device definition to process the PostScript commands
and build the blocks of text, graphics, and image components that make up a
PostScript page.

We defined this as a generator function. This generator will process the results of
the self.doc.get_pages() generator function. Since get_pages() is lazy, our
page_iter() should also be lazy. Each page is processed separately, avoiding the
overhead of trying to process the entire document at once.

The internal details of each page object will be rather complex, since each individual
PostScript command is left more-or-less intact. We'll add some text aggregation rules
to this to create more meaningful blocks of text. For now, however, we created a
subclass that extends the parent class to add a feature.

Here's an example of using this class to extract each page from a document.

```python
with Miner_Page(filename) as miner:
    count= 0
    for page in miner.page_iter():
        count += 1
        print(count, page.mediabox)
    print( "{count} pages".format_map(vars()))
```

[99]

Dredging up History

We dumped a little bit of page information from each page of the document. The `mediabox` attribute shows the rectangle that defines the size of the page.

PDF documents can include fill-in-the-blanks forms. In the case of form processing, the `annots` attribute will have details of the values filled in before the document was saved.

Getting text data from a document

We'll need to add some more features to our class definition so that we can extract meaningful, aggregated blocks of text. We'll need to add some layout rules and a text aggregator that uses the rules and the raw page to create aggregated blocks of text.

We'll override the `init_device()` method to create a more sophisticated device. Here's the next subclass, built on the foundation of the `Miner_Page` and `Miner` classes:

```
from pdfminer.converter import PDFPageAggregator
from pdfminer.layout import LAParams
class Miner_Layout(Miner_Page):
    def __init__(self, *args, **kw):
        super().__init__(*args, **kw)
    def init_device(self, resource_manager, **params):
        """Return an PDFPageAggregator as a device."""
        self.layout_params = LAParams(**params)
        return PDFPageAggregator(resource_manager, laparams=self.
layout_params)
    def page_iter(self):
        """Yields a LTPage object for each page in the document."""
        for page in super().page_iter():
            layout = self.device.get_result()
            yield layout
```

We provided an `__init__()` method that accepts all positional and keyword arguments as `*args` and `**kw`. This method merely calls the `super().__init__()` method. This isn't necessary because the superclass `__init__()` is used by default. We've included this to help to show that nothing extra is done in the initialization for this class. This also acts a placeholder in case we do need to change the object initialization.

The `init_device()` method overrides the superclass `init_device()` and provides a different device. Instead of a simple `PDFDevice`, we provided a `PDFPageAggregator` instance. This instance is configured by the `LAParams` object, which can be customized to change the rules for recognizing blocks of text. For now, we'll stick with the default parameters, as they seem to work for many documents.

[100]

Notice that we provided an implementation of the `page_iter()` method, which extends the superclass implementation of this method. Our subclass method uses the lazy superclass version and does an additional processing step: it invokes the device's `get_result()` method. This method builds a more useful `PDFPage` object in which the page's text is collected into meaningful chunks.

Look back at the `Miner_Page` superclass and its implementation of `page_iter()`. In that class, we consumed the results of the document's `get_pages()` generator method and used the interpreter's `process_page()` method on each page. Since the `Miner_Page.page_iter()` method was a generator function and only produced pages when requested.

The `Miner_Layout` subclass provides an implementation of `page_iter()`, which is also a generator function. This will use the `superclass().page_iter()` to get page objects. It will then use the device object to refine the data structure into meaningful blocks of text. Since this class has a lazy generator based on other lazy generators, nothing is done until an object is requested. This limits processing to the minimum required to produce the text on a single page.

We can use the `with` function like this:

```
with Miner_Layout(filename) as miner:
    for page in miner.page_iter():
        print(page, len(page))
```

This shows us that each page has dozens of individual items. Most of these are blocks of text. Other items are images or graphics. If, for example, a block of text is surrounded by a box, there will be a number of line drawing objects within the page object. Fortunately, it's easy to distinguish the various kinds of objects available within a page.

Displaying blocks of text

In many cases, we'll do our object-oriented design to try and create classes that have a common interface but distinct implementations. The principle is called isomorphism. Sometimes, this is summarized as the substitution principle: we can replace an instance of one class with an instance of an isomorphic class. Since the two classes are used in have different behaviors, the results are different. Since the classes have the same interface, the programming change amounts to replacing one class name with another.

In some cases, complete isomorphism is not implemented. If two classes many similar methods but few different methods, then the programming change to use one class instead of the other may be more extensive. In some cases, we're required to use `isinstance()` to determine the class of an object so that we can use methods and attributes appropriately.

Dredging up History

A PDF document has many things besides simple text in it. The PDF Miner simply produces a list object which contains the items on a page. We'll need to use `isinstance()` to identify text separate from other items on a page. Here's a function that will simply print the text:

```
from pdfminer.layout import LTText
def show_text(filename):
    with Miner_Layout(filename) as miner:
        for page in miner.page_iter():
            for ltitem in page:
                if isinstance(ltitem, LTText):
                    print( ltitem.get_text() )
```

We used `Miner_Layout` to open a document. This means that the `page_iter()` method will provide pages that have been analyzed by the `PDFPageAggregator` object to create meaningful blocks of text. The output from this is a dump of the PDF content including page headers and page footers.

When we evaluate `show_text('compendiumfederaldatasources.pdf')`, we'll see text starting with this:

```
Compendium of Federal Data Sources to
Support Health Workforce Analysis
April 2013

Health Resources and Services Administration
Bureau of Health Professions
National Center for Health Workforce Analysis

Compendium of Federal Data Sources to Support Health Workforce
Analysis April 2013

1
```

The `1` at the end is the page number. This is the kind of junk text that we'll need to filter out.

As we look further into the document, we find this:

```
Table 1-Summary List: Federal Data Sources for Health Workforce
Analysis

Data Source

Federal Agency Website

Data Collection
```

[102]

```
Method

Unit of
Analysis

Potential Use
in Health
Workforce
Analysis
```

The content of the table has been broken down into cells and the cells have been emitted in a potentially confusing order. The problem gets worse. Here's where the data starts to get interesting:

```
http://www.ah
rq.gov/data/h
cup/
```

We really want the list of URLs so that we can get the primary data to analyze the workforce. But the URLs are all chopped up to cram them into a table.

We have some elements of the solution:

- If we purge the \n characters, we'll be able to track down the URLs buried in the content. But will we have enough context to know what they mean?
- If we do a little clever layout exploration, we might be able to put the cells of the table into a proper grid and recover some context clues.
- Also, this is a summary table. We can also try to locate the URLs deeper in the body of the document.

If we can recover the original grid layout, we might be able to gather useful context information from the table. We'll look at the **bbox (bounding box)** attribute of each item.

Understanding tables and complex layouts

In order to work successfully with PDF documents, we need to process some parts of the page geometry. For some kinds of running text, we don't need to worry about where the text appears on the page. But for tabular layouts, we're forced to understand the gridded nature of the display. We're also forced to grapple with the amazing subtlety of how the human eye can take a jumble of letters on a page and resolves them into meaningful rows and columns.

Dredging up History

It doesn't matter now, but as we move forward it will become necessary to understand two pieces of PDF trivia. First, coordinates are in points, which are about 1/72 of an inch. Second, the origin, (0,0), is the lower-left corner of the page. As we read down the page, the *y* coordinate decreases toward zero.

A PDF page will be a sequence of various types of layout objects. We're only interested in the various subclasses of LTText.

The first thing we'll need is a kind of filter that will step through an iterable sequence of LTText objects; it will reject those before the first trigger, it will yield those after the first trigger, and it will stop when it gets to the second trigger. This sounds like a small function with some for statements and if statements.

In order to keep this function simple, we'll define a function that iterates through all the LTText objects on a page of the document. It's a tiny modification to the previous show_text() function:

```
def layout_iter(page):
    for ltitem in page:
        if isinstance(ltitem, LTText):
            yield ltitem
```

This function requires a Miner_Layout function for a given document file. It must be given a page from the layout's page_iter() method. Within each page it will iterate through each item. If the item is an instance of LTText, then it is produced as the result of this generator. All of the other items are silently rejected.

While some parts of a document appear to span pages, that's entirely something we've learned to do while being taught to read. The text ends on one page. There may be additional text like page footers and page headers. The text then resumes on a subsequent page. The connection between pages is a conclusion we draw from a well-designed document.

We can use this function in a for statement like this:

```
>>> with Miner_Layout('compendiumfederaldatasources.pdf') as miner:
...     for page in miner.page_iter():
...         text= list( layout_iter(page) )
...         break
>>> text[0]
    <LTTextBoxHorizontal(0) 72.024,630.355,539.390,713.369 'Compendium
of Federal Data Sources to \nSupport Health Workforce Analysis  \
nApril 2013 \n'>
>>> text[-1]
<LTTextLineHorizontal 565.900,760.776,568.150,768.957 ' \n'>
```

Chapter 4

We created a `Miner_Layout` object and assigned it to the miner variable. We retrieved the first page from this document, and then built a list from our `layout_iter()` generator function. This list object will have each text object from a given page. The output shows us that we created a proper generator function that produces only text items.

This function also acts like a filter. It's rejecting non-text objects and passing the `LTText` objects. We could use the built-in `filter()` function to do this. We can transform a `for-if` structure into a `filter()` function by taking the condition out of the if statement and making it a separate function, or a lambda object.

The resulting expression would look like this:

```
list( filter(lambda ltitem: isinstance(ltitem, LTText), page) )
```

While this is shorter than the `layout_iter()` function, it may be more confusing. It can also be somewhat harder to tweak as we learn more about the data. Since both the `layout_iter()` function and the `filter()` expression are equivalent, the choice of which one to use depends on clarity and expressiveness.

The output shows us that our text items have names like `LTTextBoxHorizontal`. This is a subclass of `LTText`. We won't care about the precise subclass. All of the subclasses of `LTText` are—it turns out—polymorphic for our purposes. We don't need to use the `isinstance()` function to distinguish among the subclasses.

The output also shows us that some text items will have just spaces and newlines, and can be safely ignored. It appears that we need to filter the content as well as filtering the structure of the resulting objects.

Writing a content filter

We'll need to do some filtering of the content. The previous `layout_iter()` filter looked at the class of each item on a page. It passed objects of some classes—specifically any subclass of `LTText` and it rejected objects of all other classes.

We'll need two filters to look at the content of the text, and reject specific blocks of text. First, we need to reject empty blocks of text. This function can follow the same template as the `layout_iter()` function. We'll call this `reject_empty()`, since it rejects empty blocks of text:

```
def reject_empty(text_iter):
    for ltitem in text_iter:
        if ltitem.get_text().strip():
            yield ltitem
```

Dredging up History

This will iterate through all of the layout items on a given page. If the text—when stripped—still has some content left, we'll continue to process this. If nothing is left after applying the `strip()` method, we'll silently reject this whitespace.

We can rebuild this to use the `filter()` function. We would create a lambda object out of the condition, `ltitem.get_text().strip()`. We'll leave that rewrite as an exercise for the agent who needs to know all of their software design alternatives.

We can also write this function using a generator expression:

```
def reject_empty(text_iter):
    return (ltitem for ltitem in text_iter
        if ltitem.get_text().strip())
```

This expression yields text items from the `text_iter` variable if there's content after the item has been stripped of whitespace. A generator expression combines the iterating capability of a `for` statement with the conditional processing of an `if` statement. When the result is a simple expression (like the `ltitem` variable), this kind of compact notation can express the intent very clearly.

When we look at stray text scattered around the page, a simple filter becomes awkward. We have several things we want to get rid of, and they form a very short list. We need a function like this:

```
def reject_footer(text_iter):
    for ltitem in text_iter:
        txt = ltitem.get_text().strip()
        if txt in ('5', '6'): continue
        if txt ==  'Compendium of Federal Data Sources to Support
Health Workforce Analysis April 2013':
            continue
        if txt == 'Table 1-Summary List: Federal Data Sources for
Health Workforce Analysis':
            continue
        yield ltitem
```

We've identified four specific strings that we don't want to see: page numbers, page footer, and table header. Yes, the function is misnamed: three-quarters of the junk text are footers, but one-quarter is actually a table header. When we see any of these strings, we continue processing the `for` statement, essentially rejecting these text items. All other strings, however, are yielded as the result from this filter. We could try to finesse this into a slightly more sophisticated filter or generator expression. However, we always seem to turn up another odd-ball piece of text to ignore. Leaving this filter as an easy-to-edit function seems to provide the best approach.

We've seen three ways of filtering here:

- Generator functions using the `yield` statement
- The `filter()` function using functions or lambda objects
- Generator expressions using (*expression* `for` *variable* `in` *source* `if` *condition*)

Since they're all functionally identical, the choice of which one to use depends on clarity.

Filtering the page iterator

We don't want to extract text for the entire document. We only want to extract text from the two pages that have the relevant table. This calls for a slightly more sophisticated filter. Clearly, we can filter page numbers in `range(5,7)`. (Remember, Python interprets this as $5 \le p < 7$: the start value is included, and the stop value is excluded.)

However, once we're past page seven, there's no reason to continue processing. So, we have a slightly more complex filter function.

```
def between( start, stop, page_iter ):
    for page in page_iter:
        if start <= page.pageid < stop:
            yield page
        if stop <= page.pageid:
            break
```

This function's input must be the kinds of data produced by a `Miner_Layout` object. This can be used to "wrap" the `page_iter()` method and yield only pages in the desired range, stopping when the range is finished.

While we could try to use this as an equivalent, this version doesn't stop early.

```
filter( lambda page: start <= page.pageid < stop, page_iter )
```

This alternative would process all pages, wasting a bit of time.

We'd use this as follows:

```
with Miner_Layout('compendiumfederaldatasources.pdf') as miner:
    for page in between(5, 7, miner.page_iter()):
        sort_by_yx( page )
```

This will apply some function named `sort_by_yx()` to each page in the given range. This demonstrates the general context we'll use to extract useful data from the larger PDF document structure. We'll look at the `sort_by_yx()` function next.

[107]

Dredging up History

Exposing the grid

We've seen how we can reject non-text, empty blocks of text, and junk text from a page. We've even seen how to reject the wrong pages. Let's see what's available on the page. We want to grab each block of text and put them into a list organized by their row and column based on the y and x coordinates of the bounding box. Generally, it looks like top-left portion of each box in this document seems to be nicely positioned within the grid.

We'll use a design pattern called the wrap-sort-unwrap design. We'll create a small 3-tuple from each layout item: (y, x, item). The item is the original item. The y and x coordinates are attributes extracted from the item's bbox attribute. We've wrapped the original item just for the purposes of sorting. We can then unwrap the item to recover a sequence of layout items in a proper sequence from top-left to bottom-right of the overall grid.

Here's how we can do this:

```
def sort_by_yx(page):
    base_text = reject_footer( reject_empty( layout_iter(page) ) )
    x0= lambda bbox : int(bbox[0])
    y1= lambda bbox : int(bbox[3])
    rows = [(y1(ltitem.bbox), x0(ltitem.bbox), ltitem) for ltitem in
base_text]
    rows.sort(key=lambda triple: (-triple[0],triple[1]))
    for y, x, ltitem in rows:
        print( y, x, repr(ltitem.get_text()) )
```

This function combines our various filters into a chain. First we'll use the layout_ iter() filter to winnow our all by LTText items; then we'll use reject_empty() to filter out text with no meaningful content; and finally we'll use reject_footer() to reject page numbers, page footers, and a table header that aren't meaningful.

We've created two lambda objects, x0 and y1, to pick items out of the bbox tuple and apply the int() conversion to the values. This kind of named lambda allows us to use y1(ltitem.bbox) instead of int(ltitem.bbox[3]). When working with tuples, it's often difficult to remember which position a useful item is in. Using lambdas like this is one way to clarify the positions in use.

In this case, bbox has four values, x0, y0, x1, y2, that comprise two sets of coordinates: (x0,y0) is the left-bottom corner and (x1,y1) is the right-top corner. We want the left-top coordinates, so we use x0 and y2.

We've used a list comprehension to build the rows object. This comprehension will create the list of three-tuples that have the y and x coordinates as well as the layout item, ltitem, of interest.

[108]

Chapter 4

Once we've build the `rows` object, we can sort it and display the results. The sort must be in decreasing order of y coordinate and increasing order of x coordinate. We've stolen a pretty clever trick of negating one number to put the y values into decreasing order

The details are very interesting. We'll show some highlights of the output. Here are the first two rows of the table:

```
703 72 'Data Source \n'
703 151 'Federal Agency Website \n'
703 310 'Data Collection \nMethod \n'
703 389 'Unit of \nAnalysis \n'
703 469 'Potential Use \nin Health \nWorkforce \nAnalysis \n'
643 72 'Healthcare \nCost and \nUtilization \nProject (HCUP) \n'
643 151 'Agency for \nHealthcare \nResearch and \nQuality (AHRQ), \
nU.S. DHHS  \nAgency for \nHealthcare \nResearch and \nQuality (AHRQ),
\nU.S. DHHS  \n'
643 239 'http://www.ah\nrq.gov/data/h\ncup/ \n'
643 310 'health claims \ndata \n'
643 389 'health care \nencounter \n'
643 469 'health care \ndemand \n'
```

What we see is that the x coordinates step nicely across the page. Since PDFs are measured in points, about 1/72 of an inch, position 72 is one inch from the edge. We can similarly see that the top-most row is about 9.76 inches from the bottom of the page.

Once we've seen all of the coordinates on the page, we can easily create a mapping x values to column numbers and y values to row numbers. This can be done after seeing all of the rows so that the complete set of unique coordinate values are known.

The second page has a number of anomalies. The first is the text which is present after the awkward page break that occurred before the last line of a cell. This leads to a jumble of text for the first row of the second page of the table. Some of that jumble is an artifact of how PDFMiner3k is valiantly trying to assemble text blocks for us.

The next anomaly on the second page is this:

```
537 73 'Medicare \nClaims Data \n'
537 240 'http://www.c\nms.gov/Resea\nrch-Statistics-\nData-and-\
nSystems/Rese\narch-\nStatistics-\nData-and-\nSystems.html  \nhttp://
www.c\nms.gov/Resea\nrch-Statistics-\nData-and-\nSystems/Rese\narch/
MCBS/in\ndex.html \nhttp://www.c\nms.gov/Regul\nations-and-\nGuidance/
HIP\nAA-\nAdministrative\n-\nSimplification/\nNationalProvId\
nentStand/inde\nx.html \nhttp://arf.hrsa\n.gov/  \n'
537 311 'health claims \ndata \n'
```

[109]

Dredging up History

```
537 391 'health care \nencounter \n'
537 470 'provider supply; \nhealth care \ndemand; health \ncare access
\n'
```

The third column, positioned at (240, 537) has a host of \n characters in it. Looking carefully for `http`, we can see that it has at least four URLs jammed into it. The subsequent rows have no data in the third column. This is very difficult to decompose.

Clearly, the `LAParams` settings have lead the `PDFPageAggregator` algorithms to mash the content of four table cells together. This is likely because they are so close that they appear to be one giant text block. We need to tweak the `LAParams` values to gently pry this text apart.

Making some text block recognition tweaks

Adjusting the `LAParams` settings is fraught with peril. This is not wonderfully well documented. Interested agents can—and should—read the relevant code form the `pdfminer.layout` module. It's instructive in that it shows good programming practices, and the consequences of having very little documentation.

This module is highly configurable and can be used to extract meaningful content from a variety of documents. However, it requires some care to be sure that the parameters continue to provide useful results.

We'll adjust the `LAParams` settings like this:

```
with Miner_Layout('compendiumfederaldatasources.pdf',
        char_margin=2.0, line_margin=0.25) as miner:
    print( miner.layout_params )
    for page in between(5, 7, miner.page_iter()):
        print( "page", page.pageid )
        sort_by_yx(page)
```

We've provided two keyword parameters to the `Miner_Layout` constructor. These will be collected into the `kw` dictionary. From there, they're given to the superclass, which will use to initialize the `LAParams function` when creating the device in the `init_device()` method. Changing the line margin will change the rules for running blocks of text together and will lead to less jumble in the output.

When we see these results, the anomaly on the second page after location 537 73 'Medicare \nClaims Data \n' has disappeared. We've disentangled the four lines of text by reducing the margin between text blocks. A quick scan shows that this looks like something we can repackage into a more useful form.

Chapter 4

Emitting CSV output

We want to get to a plain text file that we can use as a simple reference. We can read this file to get the URLs and then use those URLs to build up a library of actionable intelligence. CSV format files are perhaps the greatest invention for agents and analysts. They're timeless and don't require sophisticated software to process them. We can load them into spreadsheets and reformat them to be pretty, but the underlying data is columns of pure, sweet text.

We'll need to make some small changes to our current functions so that we can write CSV files instead of printing debugging and diagnostic information to the console.

The first thing we need to do is chop the `sort_by_yx()` function into two parts. The function should be shortened to return the sorted list of (`y`, `x`, `ltitem`) tuples and do nothing more. A new function, `print_yxtext()`, should accept the list of three-tuples as parameter and iterate through the rows printing `y`, `x`, and the value of `ltitem.get_text()`.

Once we've chopped the original `sort_by_yx()` function apart, we can write a new function that accepts a list of three-tuples as a parameter and builds individual CSV rows. We note that the *x* values increment across a row and then jump back down at the beginning of the next row. We can use this to separate the cells of each spreadsheet row:

```
def csv_yxtext(rows):
    max_x = 0
    line = []
    for y, x, ltitem in rows:
        if x < max_x:
            yield line
            line= []
        line.append( ltitem.get_text().replace('\n','').strip() )
        max_x= x
    yield line
```

We've started with an empty line and a maximum x value, `max_x`, set to an initial value of zero. As we look at each cell, we'll compare the cells x with `max_x`. If the cells x is less than `max_x`, we've started a new line. We can emit the old line. We always append the cells text to the current line and save the maximum value of x seen so far in `max_x`. After we emit the final line, we'll have a list of (`y`, `x`, `ltitem`) in individual rows of `ltitems`.

[111]

Dredging up History

The result is a respectable CSV file that can (almost) be used without any further manual tweaks. There are two rows that require special attention. We can simply edit those two rows. One row has a stray block of CDC, U.S. DHH, and the other row has a stray line of `x.html`.

We can try to fine-tune the `LAParams` settings to keep the stray `x.html` block of text properly connected to the cell above it. This leads to a machine learning sort of solution. We will consider this table as a training set of data. We iterate through multiple `LAParams` settings until we find values for which the training set passes the test of reconstructing all but one cell perfectly.

(The other damaged cell with CDC, U.S. DHH can't be rebuilt because it spans pages. Don't try to fix this by adjusting the `LAParams` settings.)

Perfectionists will note that the x value in these two cases provides a hint as to what's going on. The row didn't start with an x value of 72 or 73, it started with a larger number that maps to a column that's not column one.

Rather than simply assume that a low number starts a new row, we could see if the low number means that we've got text that should get appended to a particular column within the previous row. We can see that an x value of 152 maps to column two and an x value of 240 maps to column three. This little cleanup logic might be simpler than using machine learning to tweak the `LAParams` settings.

This little cleanup is quite challenging to address in a perfectly general way. Another table will of course have other column positions. A more general solution will gather a sorted list of x coordinates to map a position to a column number. For some small things like this, it might be easier to edit the CSV than it is to edit the code that rebuilds the CSV.

Summary

We saw how we can tease meaningful information out of a PDF document. We assembled a core set of tools to extract outlines from documents, summarize the pages of a document, and pull the text from each page. We also discussed how we can analyze a table or other complex layout to reassemble meaningful information from that complex layout.

We used a very clever Python design pattern called wrap-sort-unwrap to decorate text blocks with coordinate information, and then sort it into the useful top-to-bottom and left-to-right positions. Once we had the text properly organized, we could unwrap the meaningful data and produce useful output.

We also discussed two other important Python design patterns: the context manager and the filter. We used object-oriented design techniques to create a hierarchy of context managers that simplify our scripts to extract data from files. The filter concept has three separate implementations: as a generator expression, as a generator function, and using the built-in `filter()` function.

In the next chapter, we'll look at data collection at the gadget level. We'll dig into the ways that we can use a small device like an Arduino or a Raspberry Pi as part of the Internet of Things (IoT). We can attach controls and sensors to these devices and gather data from a wide variety of sources.

5
Data Collection Gadgets

We've looked at gathering intelligence from web server logs, from the social network, and from hard-to-examine PDF files. In this chapter, we'll see how we can gather data from the real world—the space that isn't inside our computers. This can be poetically termed **meatspace** to distinguish it from the cyberspace of networked computers.

There are a large number of small, programmable devices with sophisticated network interfaces, processes, and memory. We'll focus on the Arduino family of processors as a way to gather data for analysis. Some agents will prefer to use other processors because they're less expensive, more sophisticated, or have different programming language support.

Our goal is to build our own gadget using a simple sensor. We can easily find numerous online shops that sell a variety of sensors. We can even find kits with a collection of different kinds of sensors. Some agents will prefer to shop for individual sensors on a project-by-project basis. This trades upfront cash outlay against incremental transportation costs as more parts are ordered.

We'll look at a specific sensor for measuring distance. It's got a relatively simple interface, and it requires some care to calibrate it properly. Calibration means that we'll need to do some careful preliminary data gathering before we can use the device operationally.

This chapter will cover a number of topics:

- We'll start with a background briefing on Arduino basics.
- This will help us organize a shopping list of parts that we'll need in order to build a working sensor. We'll look at doing all of our shopping at once versus buying parts as we need them.
- We'll look at Arduino sketches to control the digital output pins. We'll start with the traditional "hello world" sketch that blinks an LED.

Data Collection Gadgets

- We'll look at some hardware design considerations regarding current and voltage levels. This will help us avoid frying our parts with too much power. We'll use small Python programs to design the resistors that protect our LEDs.

- We'll look at how we put some parts into a breadboard to create a working gadget.

- The Arduino programming language will take some effort to learn. It's not Python, and field agents will see the need to learn multiple programming languages.

- Once we've seen the basics of the Arduino language, we can create a much better blinking light.

- We'll leverage the blinking light design to poll a push-button. The polling technique we'll use allows us to build responsive gadgets.

- Once we've seen the basics of the Arduino language and connecting parts with a breadboard, we're ready to create our data collection device.

- We can use the USB interface to send collected data back to our computer. We can then use Python programs to analyze the data. The first analysis job will be to calibrate our sensor.

- Based on our Python-based analysis, we'll create a simple software filter algorithm to reduce the noise in our sensor. This will allow us to collect high-quality data for subsequent analysis with Python.

We won't address some of the final construction and assembly issues for gadgets. There are many places that will create printed circuit boards: an agent can attach parts to create a robust device this way. There are some places that can even assemble boards given detailed engineering specifications. **CadSoft**, for example, offers the Eagle software and has PCB fabrication partners that can build boards. Visit http://www.cadsoftusa.com. Also, visit http://fab.fritzing.org/fritzing-fab for another software package that can help design the boards that go into sophisticated gadgets.

Background briefing: Arduino basics

The history of the Arduino combines art and technology. For more information, visit http://aliciagibb.com/wp-content/uploads/2013/01/New-Media-Art-Design-and-the-Arduino-Microcontroller-2.pdf.

More relevant background will come from the *Getting Started with Arduino* by author *Massimo Banzi*, which is the standard starter book. Also, most publishers, like Packt Publishing, have dozens of books on Arduino. We won't duplicate any of that material. We will show how data collection and analysis works with customized gadgets.

Chapter 5

The Arduino supports the idea of physical computing—computing that interacts with the real world through sensors and actuators. To this end, the Arduino board has a processor, some pins that the processor can sense, and some pins that the processor can control. There's also a small reset button and a USB connector, plus miscellaneous parts like a crystal for the clock and a connector for power that can be used instead of the USB connector.

Each of the Arduino boards is slightly different. The older Arduino Uno is typical, so we'll look at that as representative of the various kinds of boards available.

First, and most important, some of the terms are metaphoric. The term pin for instance, often refers to the leg or stiff wire connector to an electronic component. Some boards will have pin connectors bristling around the edges. For most things there's a male and a female part to the connection. The Arduino Uno board, for example, has a ring of plastic sockets into which a pin can fit and make a secure, reliable electrical connection. These sockets are called pins even though they're clearly sockets into which pins must be inserted.

Around the edge of the board, there are 14 digital I/O pins. These are capable of sensing a completed circuit or providing board-level voltage. We often use these to detect the state of external buttons or switches. We might also use the output feature for status lights.

There are six analog input pins. These can detect from 0 to 5 volts. The exact voltage level is available to software as an input. This is summarized as Analog-to-Digital (A/D or A to D) conversion.

There are six analog output pins. This can produce from 0 to 5 volts under control of software. These aren't separate pins on the Arduino; these are separate use cases for six of the digital pins. If we want to use analog output, we have to sacrifice some digital capabilities. We can call this Digital-to-Analog (D/A or D to A) conversion.

Perhaps most importantly, there's a serial/USB interface that we can use via the Arduino IDE or via standalone Python applications. We'll use the USB connector to download software to the Arduino. We'll also use this to extract data from the Arduino for calibration and analysis.

Additionally, there's a 2.1 mm power connector that can be used to power a board instead of the USB connector. We can use this to run an Arduino separately from any computer. This expects 9V DC; the 2.1 mm connector should have a positive tip. Some vendors sell handy boxes that hold a 9V batter and have the required connector already attached.

[117]

Data Collection Gadgets

Organizing a shopping list

In order to build Arduino gadgets, we'll need an Arduino board. We described the Arduino Uno, but any board from the Arduino family will work nicely. Arduino's Entry-Level products are the focus here. The entry-level kit products include much of what we need.

It helps to have a bag of buttons, potentiometers, LEDs, and a mixed collection of resistors. A set of jumper wires are also essential. The more complex missions will require a small solderless breadboard to lay out parts.

We'll be building a data collection gadget using an infrared (IR) Range Sensor. These devices seem to be a reliable way to watch doors or windows open, and watch people come and go. This sensor is an infrared diode and detector in one tidy little package. An example is the **Sharp GP2D12** (or the more commonly-available GP2Y0A02YK0F.) It is small and it can be affixed in a variety of places. There are a number of alternatives with different distance capabilities.

Many of these distance sensors have a small mounting bracket that requires a JST 3-wire male jumper to connect from the socket to an Arduino. It's possible to find vendors who supply both parts, saving some shipping costs. Ideally, an agent can locate an Arduino starter kit plus these additional non-standard sensors from a single vendor.

A piezo buzzer (more properly a speaker) can be used to produce tones. We might use this as part of an alarm or warning in addition to LEDs.

For agents new to building gadgets, there are some nice items, also. While it is not essential to have a reliable volt-ohm meter, many gadget builders find them indispensable. It is sometimes handy to be able to examine the voltage available on a pin or check the resistance of a device. A basic meter is helpful for seeing if a battery is dead, too.

We won't start by soldering anything. Agents should be able to solder without making a terrible mess of the parts. Many of the vendors sell breakout boards onto which small parts can be soldered. These breakout boards can then be plugged into breadboards or interconnected easily with jumper wires, making it somewhat easier to make complex gadgets.

Getting it right the first time

Getting it right the first time is not the Arduino way. Any experienced agent knows that nothing ever works quite the way we expect. It helps to be flexible and responsive to a fluid situation. We write Python software to analyze and gather data because we know that flexibility is important. Last-minute changes are part of the job.

Chapter 5

The Arduino-based gadget building is no different. The voltages are low and the amount of current involved is minor. If we wire something backwards, it simply won't work. If we miscalculate a resistor, we may fry an LED. We redo our calculations, plug in a new resistor and fresh LED, and start again. The goal of the Arduino is to explore the world of interactive gadgets without concerns about expensive mistakes.

A common phrase among gadget builders is the smoke test: plug it in and see if it smokes. If there's smoke, one of the parts is fried and we'll have some debugging to do to find the misplaced wires. Since we're only talking about 5V DC and a board that requires about 25 mA of current, this only involves 0.125 Watts of power. We don't get much smoke if something does go wrong.

(For comparison, a common household appliance like a Waffle Maker runs at 110V AC, and may draw 1000 W. This represents an actual hazard as compared to an Arduino.)

Starting with the digital output pins

We'll use the digital output pins for our first mission. This will show us the basics of preparing a sketch—an Arduino program. We'll download it to an Arduino and watch it work.

The Arduino language is vaguely like Python, with some extraneous punctuation. The language is quite a bit simpler and is statically compiled into hardware-level instructions that are downloaded to the processor.

An Arduino sketch must define two functions: `setup()` and `loop()`. The `setup()` function will run just once when the board is reset. The `loop()` will be evaluated repeatedly—as often as possible—by the Arduino processor. The exact timing will vary depending on what additional tasks the processor has to engage in to manage memory and deal with the various devices. It's almost is if the Arduino has an overall piece of code that looks like this:

```
main() {
    setup();
    while(true) { loop(); }
}
```

We don't need to actually write code like this; our sketch is written as if this processing exists somewhere in the Arduino.

[119]

Data Collection Gadgets

We design our sketches to fit into the overall Arduino design pattern of one `setup()` evaluation and an infinite number of `loop()` evaluations. Because of this repetitive loop concept built-in to the Arduino, we can minimize loops in our programming.

Here's the sketch to blink an LED:

```
// Pin 13 has an internal LED connected on most Arduino boards.
const int LED = 13;
void setup() {
  pinMode(LED, OUTPUT);
}
void loop() {
  digitalWrite(LED, HIGH);
  delay(1000);
  digitalWrite(LED, LOW);
  delay(1000);
}
```

We defined a handy global variable, LED, which specifies the pin we're going to use. We'd rather not copy and paste the pin number in several places. We defined it to be an integer, and further specified that this is a constant and cannot be changed.

Around the edge of the Arduino board, the pins are labeled. On an Arduino Uno, pin 13 is often next to a socket labeled GND for ground. On many Arduinos, the pins are encased in sockets, making them easier to work with.

We've set this pin into output mode. We can set an output pin to high level (+5V) or low level (ground.) The `digitalWrite()` function changes the state of a given pin. The two literal values HIGH and LOW are predefined constants that are used to set the value of digital output pins.

Socket 13 is often connected to a small on-board LED. We don't really need any parts to see if this works. We can connect the board via the USB cable to our computer and download the sketch. We can click download to send the sketch to the Arduino. Once the download is complete, the little on-board LED should commence blinking.

This is an important first step. It's worthy of celebration. There are a number of further steps we need to take. First, we want to add our own external LED to the circuit. Second, we need to fix a design flaw in this application. While it's elegantly simple, it relies in a programming technique that doesn't work well for data gathering applications. Let's start with the hardware design considerations.

Chapter 5

Designing an external LED

Since this is our first gadget, it's essential to break out the collection of parts and create a proper external LED using a resistor to limit the voltage. The issue we have is that LEDs need only a fraction of the available voltage. We have a design issue to solve before we start frying our parts. We'll use Python functions to help us design a proper resistor.

For agents new to gadget-building, think of current as the volume of water pouring through a pipe and voltage as the pressure behind that water. High current, measured in Amperes, means water filling a big pipe: the pressure can be low even if the volume is large. Our LED will consume some of the available current to create a stream of photons. We could try to flood our LED with more current, but the device can only sip the current it needs, the rest will just flow past—unused.

An LED is a diode: it's called a semiconductor because of its behavior. It must have enough pressure to start working. Too little pressure (called Voltage) and it won't create photons. Too much pressure and things will get cooked. Sometimes, the cooking is quick and there's a little pop when the device stops working. At other times, the cooking is slow and we notice one day that the device doesn't work any more, or doesn't work properly.

Our Arduino pins produce 5.0V really reliably. Our LEDs only need 2V to 3.5V, depending on the color and they only sip about 15 mA of the available current. Different LEDs have different specifications. Each agent needs to check the specifications for the LEDs they have available. Typical values include:

- Red LEDs often need about 2.5 V to work
- Yellow LEDs may need 2.8 V
- Green LEDs typically need as much as 3.4 V

We reduce the Arduino's output voltage by adding a resistor to the circuit. Resistors are measured in a unit called Ohms, Ω, which is the ratio of voltage pressure to the volume of amps that will be sipped from the circuit. The idea is that the pipe stays the same size, but the pressure of the water filling it has been reduced by a clever kind of valve.

[121]

Data Collection Gadgets

The rule for designing a voltage limiting resistor is based on the supply voltage, V_s, compared with the desired voltage at our LED, V_led. To compute the required resistance, R, we divide the voltage by the current that will be consumed by the LED, called I_led. Here's the calculation defined as a Python function:

```
def LED_R( V_led, I_led=.015, V_s=5.0):
    """LED resistor required to reduce V_s to V_led."""
    R = (V_s-V_led)/I_led
    R = std_resistor(R)
    print( "V_s={V_s:.1f}V, V_led={V_led:.1f}V,"
        " I_led={I_led:.3f}A, R={R:.0f}Ω".format_map(vars()))
```

We defined a function with two common assumptions about LEDs in an Arduino context. The current for most LEDs, in the I_led parameter, is typically about 15mA, although bright 20 mA LEDs are popular, too. The supply voltage, in the V_s parameter, is almost always 5.0 V.

We calculate the resistance as follows:

$$R = \frac{V_s - V_{led}}{I_{led}}$$

The difference is the voltage that must be eliminated from the circuit.

Before we can start rooting in our parts box, the calculated resistance must be converted to a standard resistor value. We can then print the details of the calculation so we know which resistor to pair with the LED. The problem is that our desired resistance may not be a standard value.

Resistor values are defined by an international standard. We'll use 10 percent tolerance resistors for much of our gadget building. For this level of tolerance, each decade or power of 10 is divided into 12 steps. We can calculate the steps that make up the standard with an expression like this:

```
>>> list( round(10**(i/12),1) for i in range(12) )
[1.0, 1.2, 1.5, 1.8, 2.2, 2.6, 3.2, 3.8, 4.6, 5.6, 6.8, 8.3]
```

While this is close to the standard, our calculation isn't exact enough. Getting the standard values doesn't seem to be a simple matter of rounding—agents are encouraged to fiddle around with the calculation to see if they can reproduce the standard values.

Chapter 5

To be perfectly correct, it seems simpler to provide an explicit list of standard values for 10 percent tolerance resistors:

```
E12 = (1.0, 1.2, 1.5, 1.8, 2.2, 2.7, 3.3, 3.9, 4.7, 5.6, 6.8, 8.2)
```

Here's how we use these standard numbers. We want 2.5 V (of pressure) with 15 mA (of volume) from our 5 V Arduino, we need 166.67 Ω of resistance. Assuming the resistors we have are only accurate to about 10 percent, any resistor in the range from 150 Ω to 183.3 Ω is likely to be 166.67 Ω. Either of the standard values of 150 Ω or 180 Ω will be close enough. The 180 Ω resistor is slightly closer to the target.

We can write a small Python function that will compute the appropriate standard resistor. It looks like this:

```
def std_resistor(r, series=E12):
    # 1. What decade?
    decade= 10**(int(math.log10(r)))
    # 2. R value within the decade.
    r_d= r/decade
    # 3. What are the bracketing values?
    above= decade*min( s for s in series if s >= r_d )
    below = decade*max( s for s in series if s <= r_d )
    # 4. Pick closest value.
    if (above-r)/r <= (r-below)/r: return above
    return below
```

This function relies on the standardized series values. By default, we'll use the values from the E12 series, which are defined for resistors with 10 percent tolerance. We computed the decade as a power of 10 that we can use to scale the value down to a range from 1 to 10, and then scale the series number back up to the proper resistor value. In this example of 166.667 Ω, the decade variable will be 100. The resistance factor of 1.6 is assigned to the r_d variable.

We can find the smallest standard value which is larger than our target. We can also find the largest standard value which is smaller than our target resistance. This will give us two alternatives, which we've assigned to the variables above and below.

The final decision is to pick the value closest to the target. If the value of (above-r)/r is less than (r-below)/r, then the value assigned to the above variable is the closest standard resistor. Otherwise, we'll use the below resistor. In rare cases, our target resistance will happen to be a standard value. In this case, both the above and below variables will have the same value, and the selection between them is moot.

[123]

Assembling a working prototype

Here's a typical engineering diagram for what we're going to build. We've drawn this using the Fritzing software, hence the watermark on the diagram.

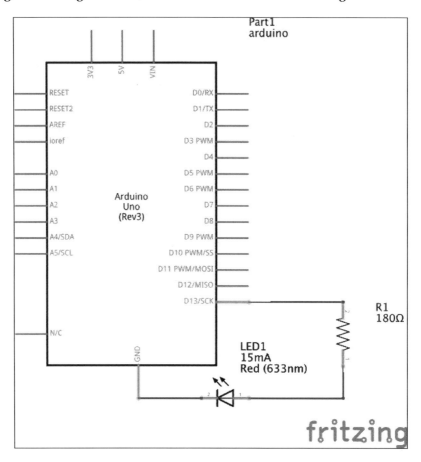

This schematic diagram shows the Arduino processor as a big rectangle with all of its pins scattered around the outside. The locations on the diagram don't reflect the physical placement of the pins; this is the conceptual organization of the board. We've shown our LED, **LED1**, as a little triangle with a line and arrows. We've annotated the LED with the current load (15 mA) and the color (633 nm). The resistor, **R1**, is a squiggle annotated with the resistance required.

An LED's positive leg (the anode) is usually longer or offset slightly or a different shape. On the diagram, the positive leg connects to the triangle side of the diode. The cathode leg (usually shorter) will connect to the Arduino GND socket.

The breadboard setup will look like this:

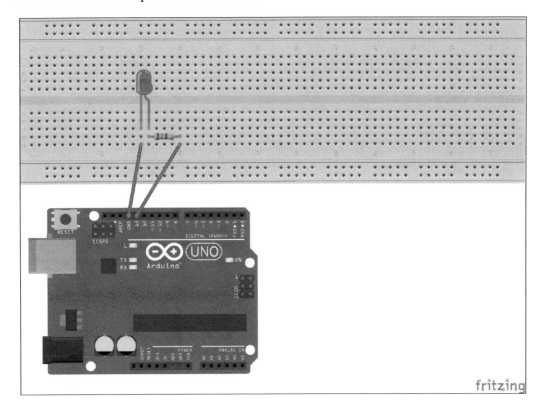

We've saved a breadboard diagram to illustrate how we'll start building things on breadboard before we attempt to create printed circuit boards. We used two jumper wires between the Arduino and the breadboard. We carefully bent the legs on a resistor and pushed them into the breadboard. We put the LED in the board so that the anode leg connects to the resistor and the cathode (or ground) leg connects to Arduino ground.

For agents new to picking out resistors, there are numerous references that explain the color coding: essentially the digits are encoded with color bands: black, brown, red, orange, yellow, green, blue, violet, grey, and white stand for the digits 0 through 9. We can consider adding the color code to our program that picks out standard resistors. The first two bands will be the two digits of the resistance, the third band is the decade, and the fourth band is generally silver for 10 percent resistors.

LEDs are diodes, and current can only flow one way. If it's plugged in backwards, it simply fails to work. This is a common error in setting up the breadboard circuit.

Data Collection Gadgets

When we see this LED blinking, we've created our first working gadget. We've written the Arduino programming sketch. We've designed and assembled the supporting hardware. Once we've created a working prototype, we can dig in more deeply to create active sensors.

Mastering the Arduino programming language

The Arduino programming language is based on C++. In Python, we use indentation to identify the body of an `if` statement, `while` statement, a function, or a class. An Arduino sketch will use {} instead of indentation.

While the {} are required syntax, almost all Arduino code that we'll see will be nicely indented as if it was Python.

Similarly, Arduino statements are separated by ; (semicolon). Python statements end at the end of the line, or the end of the matching (), [], or {}. It's challenging—at first—to remember the ; (semicolon). When we try to upload the sketch to our Arduino, the final syntax check will alert us to missing ;(semicolon).

Arduino has two kinds of comments: everything after // is a comment. This is similar to Python's # comment delimiter. Also, Arduino programs can have longer comments which begin with /* and end with */. This will often be used similarly to Python's ''' triple-quote strings. The Arduino /* */ comments can be used anywhere—even in the middle of a statement.

For simple immutable data types, the Arduino language is forced to make several distinctions that Python doesn't make. Python has a single integer type that represents all integers. The Arduino has a number of alternatives:

- `boolean`: This is a single byte that's expected to have a simple value, the literal `true` or the literal `false`.

- `char`: This is often used to store a single ASCII character. It can also be used for numbers in the range -128 to +127.

- `byte`: This is also called `unsigned char`. A single physical byte of memory holds values from 0 to 255.

- `int`: This is 2 bytes of memory, and holds values in the range of -32,768 to +32,767.

- `unsigned int` (or `word`): This is also two bytes of memory, holding values from 0 to 65,535.

[126]

- `long`: This uses 4 bytes of memory and holds values that are ±2 billion.

- `unsigned long`: This uses 4 bytes of memory and holds values from 0 to about 4 billion. One of the internal clocks on the Arduino counts time in milliseconds using `unsigned long` numbers. This gives us about 50 days of time before the internal clock resets back to zero.

Given all these kinds of integers, we'll need to predict the ranges of values we'll be using, and select a data type that will use the least amount of memory for the task at hand. Input pins, generally, provide `int` values. If we're counting events that occur about 1 time per minute, there will be no more that 1,440 in a day: too large for a `byte` or `char`. If we're using the internal clock, we're forced to work with a few `unsigned long` values.

The Arduino supports float and double-precision floating point values. We try to minimize their use, since they consume precious storage.

In some cases, we'll work with `string` values. These are simple arrays of individual characters. These are limited to the ASCII character set, so we'll only have 127 distinct characters available. In later missions, we'll send string-encoded data from our Arduino to our computer.

Unlike Python, all Arduino variables are associated with a data type. When we create a variable, we must also state what type of data will be used with that variable. We'll often see statements like this:

```
int sensor = digitalRead( SOMEPIN );
```

We've defined a `sensor` variable that must hold `int` values. We also used the `digitalRead()` function to set this variable the current status of some input pin.

Using the arithmetic and comparison operators

We have several common arithmetic operators available in the Arduino language: `+`, `-`, `*`, `/`, and `%`. In the unlikely event we need to raise a number to a power, there's a `pow()` function available. Arduino doesn't offer different division operators: if we need to do true division, we'll have to explicitly convert from an `int` value to a `float` or a `double` value.

The Arduino language uses `&`, `|`, `~`, `>>`, and `<<` exactly like Python. These operators are performing bit-by-bit operations on integer values. We can do things like this:

```
boolean b2= (a & 0x02) >> 1;
```

Data Collection Gadgets

This will extract the second bit of an integer value in the variable a. It will define a variable b2, and assign the new value to that variable.

The Arduino language has operators like Python's and, or, and not Boolean operators. In Arduino, these logical operators are spelled &&, ||, and !. These are shorter than Python's operators and look confusingly like the bit-manipulation operators.

The Arduino comparison operators are the same as Python's comparisons. Python allows us to use 2 <= a < 10 to combine two comparisons into a single tidy expression. We cannot use this shortcut in Arduino, and we must use (2 <= a) && (a < 10).

Arduino also offers ++ and -- operators. These have fairly subtle semantics, making them easy to misuse. We suggest that ++ be used only in the context of a for statement. We'll look at the Arduino for statement next.

Using common processing statements

The Arduino language has a variety of processing statements. There's potential for confusion when trying to create a mapping from one language to another language. We'll point out some of the similarities between the languages, and try to use the Arduino features that are most similar to Python.

Arduino has an assignment statement that's very similar to Python's. Note that we must define a variable's type before we can use the variable. It's common to see variables defined outside the loop() and setup() functions:

```
int BUTTON_IN = 3;
void setup() {
    pinMode(BUTTON_IN, INPUT);
}
```

We defined the type of the variable named BUTTON_IN, and assigned an initial value of 3. Inside the setup() function, we've use the pinMode() function to use this pin for input.

Arduino offers us augmented assignment statements: +=, -=, |=, and so on, so that we can perform a calculation which updates an existing variable. We might have something like this:

```
counter += 1;
```

[128]

Chapter 5

For decision-making, Python has an `if` statement: this starts with an `if` clause, has an unlimited number of `elif` clauses and an optional final `else` clause. We can build a wide-variety of conditional processing with this flexible statement.

The Arduino language has two variations on the conditional statement:

- `if` with `else if` clauses and an `else` clause. Note that `()` are required around the condition and `{}` are required around the indented body.

- `switch` statement with `case` alternatives.

The Arduino `if` statement—except for minor syntax differences—parallels the Python `if` statement. For this reason, we strongly encourage using the Arduino `if` statement and avoiding the `switch` statement. While there may be some possible advantages to the `switch` statement, the misuse of `break` statements in each `case` can lead to endless debugging. It's easier to avoid using it.

We might see this in Arduino programming:

```
if( push >= 2000 ) {
  // 2 second press.
  digitalWrite( BUTTON_LED, HIGH );
}
else if ( push >= 500 ) {
  // 0.5 sec press.
  digitalWrite( BUTTON_LED, LOW );
}
else {
  // too short.
}
```

This is similar to a Python `if-elif-else` statement. It includes the `()` and `{}` as required by the Arduino language. It includes `;` at the end of statements as well. Note that we don't have a `pass` statement in the Arduino language because we're allowed to have empty `{}`.

There are a number of looping statements. We'll look at these in the next section. We've seen enough of the language to create a better blinking LED. Once we've looked at that, we can start to gather data more seriously.

[129]

Data Collection Gadgets

Hacking and the edit, download, test and break cycle

The Arduino development cycle is a similar to the Python development cycle. In Python, we have the `>>>` interactive prompt, allowing us to do experimentation. We don't have this available for writing Arduino programs. When we're done experimenting at Python's `>>>` prompt, our development forms an edit-test-break cycle: we edit a script, test it, and fix anything that breaks.

The essential life-cycle on the Arduino has an extra step; we'll call this the Edit-Compile-Test-Break cycle:

- We'll create or modify our sketch in the Arduino IDE (or perhaps in the Fritzing code tab).

- We'll download this to our board. This will compile the sketch, reporting any syntax errors. If the sketch is valid, it will be transferred; the board will automatically reset and start operating.

- We'll try to use the board to see if it works. We'll observe the LEDs, or we'll push the buttons, turn the knobs, or we'll wave our hand in front of the distance sensor. The idea is to exercise all of the features until we either break the software, or we feel that it's fit for use.

- If something did break, we'll fix it by changing the hardware components or writing different software. In some cases, things will work, but we'll have an idea for a new feature, restarting the cycle for the next version of our gadget.

In some cases, our software will behave badly and we'll struggle to see what went wrong. The Arduino serial interface is very helpful for this. We can use the Arduino `Serial` interface to write on the USB device; the Arduino IDE can capture this data using the serial interface monitor. We can also use Python's `pyserial` interface to collect this data. This can help diagnose problems turned by during the test step.

Seeing a better blinking light

The core blinking light sketch uses a `delay(1000)` to essentially stop all work for 1 second. If we want to have a more responsive gadget, this kind of delay can be a problem. This design pattern is called **Busy Waiting** or **Spinning**: we can do better.

The core `loop()` function is executed repeatedly. We can use the `millis()` function to see how long it's been since we turned the LED on or turned the LED off. By checking the clock, we can interleave LED blinking with other operations. We can gather sensor data as well as check for button presses, for example.

Here's a way to blink an LED that allows for additional work to be done:

```
const int LED=13; // the on-board LED
void setup() {
    pinMode( LED, OUTPUT );
}
void loop() {
    // Other Work goes here.
    heartbeat();
}
// Blinks LED 13 once per second.
void heartbeat() {
  static unsigned long last= 0;
  unsigned long now= millis();
  if (now - last > 1000) {
    digitalWrite( LED, LOW );
    last= now;
  }
  else  if (now - last > 900) {
    digitalWrite( LED, HIGH );
  }
}
```

We used the `const` keyword on the LED variable. This formalizes the notion that this variable should not be changed anywhere else in the sketch.

The `setup()` function sets pin 13 to be in output mode. We can then energize and de-energize this pin to blink an LED. The `loop()` function can do some work—like read sensors—as well as execute the `heartbeat()` function.

The `heartbeat()` function defines the `last` variable marked with `static`. The keyword `static` in Arduino is related to the `@staticmethod` descriptor used in Python. This static annotation means that the value of the variable is not reset each time the function is evaluated. Compare this with the variable `now`, which is recreated every time the function is executed. This alternative to `static` is called automatic—a new variable is created and initialized each time the function is executed.

We've created a kind of timeline based on the `millis()` clock. There are three ranges of values:

- `0 <= now-last < 900`: We want to leave the LED pin set to LOW.
- `900 <= now-last < 1000`: We set LED pin set to HIGH.
- `1000 <= now-last`: We'll reset the `last` variable and also set the pin to LOW.

The range of values can be changed to modify the duty cycle of the LED. We've defined the rules to be 90 percent off and 10 percent on.

Data Collection Gadgets

Simple Arduino sensor data feed

A button is not the simplest kind of sensor to read. While the concept is simple, there's an interesting subtlety to reading a button. The problem is that buttons bounce: they make some intermittent contact before they make a final, solid connection.

There's a simplistic way to debounce that involves a **Busy Waiting** design. We'll avoid this and show a somewhat more sophisticated debounce algorithm. As with the LED blinking, we'll rely on the millis() function to see how long the button has stayed in a given state.

To debounce, we'll need to save the current state of the button. When the button is pressed, the signal on the input pin will become HIGH and we can save the time at which this leading edge event occurred. When the button is released, the signal will go back to LOW. We can subtract the two times to compute the duration. We can use this to determine if this was a proper press, just a bounce, or even a long press-and-hold event.

The function looks like this:

```
const int BUTTON_IN= 7;
unsigned long debounce() {
  static unsigned long rise_time= 0;
  static int button_state= LOW;
  int probe= digitalRead( BUTTON_IN );
  // Leading edge.
  if( probe == HIGH && button_state == LOW ) {
    rise_time= millis();
    button_state= probe;
    return 0;
  }
  unsigned long duration= millis()-rise_time;
  // Trailing edge.
  if( probe == LOW && button_state == HIGH ) {
    button_state= probe;
    return duration;
  }
  return 0;
}
```

We used two static variables to save the previous button state in the button_state variable and the time at which the button was pressed in the rise_time variable. The signal from the pin rose from LOW to HIGH, so we decided to call this time value rise_time.

[132]

We set the `probe` variable to the current state of the pin to which the button is connected. When this is HIGH, the button has been pressed (or is bouncing). When this is LOW, the button has been released. The expression `probe == HIGH && button_state == LOW` reflects the state change when the button is first pressed and starts bouncing. When this happens, we'll change the button state and save the value of `millis()`. We return a value of 0 because we don't yet know the duration of the button press.

The expression `probe == LOW && button_state == HIGH` will be true when the button has been released (or finished a bounce.) We can reset the button state and return the duration since the button was pressed. If this is a number that's greater than 10, it's generally a solid push of the button, not a bounce. A value of about 100 would be a full 1/10th of a second push. A value of 2,000 would be a long 2-second push-and-hold.

We'll use this function in the `loop()` like this:

```
const int BUTTON_LED= 8;
void loop() {
    static int button = LOW;
    unsigned long push= debounce();
    if ( push >= 10 ) {
        // change button LED from HIGH to LOW
        if( button == LOW ) { button = HIGH; }
        else { button = LOW; }
        digitalWrite( BUTTON_LED, button );
    }
    heartbeat();
}
```

This version of the `loop()` function references the `heartbeat()` function shown previously. This will provide some visual confirmation that the sketch is running. If we measure a button press of more than 1/100th of a second, it's not a bounce and we'll make a change to an LED. If the LED was previously LOW, we'll switch the LED to HIGH; otherwise, the LED must have been HIGH, so we'll switch it to LOW.

We defined a variable named BUTTON_LED to identify the LED that's being changed. The name implies that the LED has something to do with a button. HQ likes us to use the clever little tactile buttons that have an LED in the dome of the button. The package for this is very small, and doesn't easily plug into the breadboard. Agents will need to buy a breakout board for these tactile LEDs. We can solder the tactile LED button to little board along with header pins, and connect the assembly as a whole to our breadboard.

Data Collection Gadgets

The advantage of this is that we can use this LED to provide visual feedback that something is operating properly. The downside of complex gadgets is that they can fail in sometimes mysterious ways. Providing rich levels of feedback can help show that the gadget is operating properly.

The wiring schematic for a button with an LED looks like this:

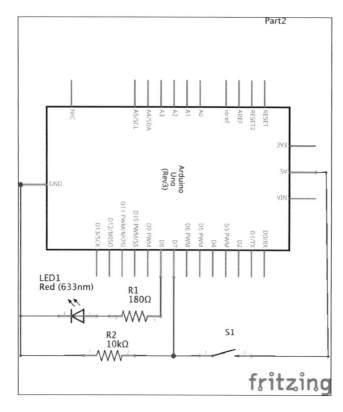

We've shown the button as **S1**. It has a rather complex circuit using a 10 KΩ resistor. This is called a pull down resistor and is required to provide a proper LOW voltage state on the input pin. For these kinds of digital devices, we can't simply leave a circuit open with no connection.

We've shown the LED, **LED1**, also. We separated these two parts in the schematic diagram. Physically, the switch and LED are both packaged as a single part. We've assumed that the tactile LED that requires only 2.5 V and therefore needs 180 Ω of resistance.

We build a responsive little device which can change state and shows an active heartbeat. We can leverage this design to do analog data collection. We can even do some preliminary analysis of the data on the Arduino board.

Collecting analog data

Our goal is to gather data from an analog range sensor. This device must be connected to one of the analog input pins. We also need to connect it to power and ground pins. According to the documentation for the GP2Y0A21YK, the sensor has three connections: Vo, GND, and Vcc. With the sensor pointing up, the left-most pin is generally Vo, the output that will connect to Arduino A0 to provide analog input. The center pin is ground, which connects to one of the Arduino GND connections. The right-most pin will be Vcc, the supply voltage that will connect to the +5 V pin on the Arduino.

Many of these devices have a little JST three-wire socket. We can buy a nice little JST three-wire jumper. The color coding of the wires on the jumper may not fit our expectations very well. We may wind up with Vcc on the black-colored wire (black is often used for ground) and the ground connection on the red-colored wire (red is often used for +5V.)

If we connect things up wrong, there will likely be a short circuit and the Arduino board will simply stop working. The green power LED on the board will fade out.

Once we have the part wired properly, we'll need to use the `analogRead()` function to gather the input from pin A0. This will be an integer value between 0 and 1024 that reflects the measured voltage level between 0 and 5 V. We can compute the actual voltage level, v, from a raw input number, s, as $v=5*s/1024$. For now, we'll just look at the raw input values.

We can collect some initial data with a very simple sketch that reads the value and writes it to the serial interface. Here's this initial sketch for reading the distance device:

```
int samples[4];
void gather_data() {
  for( int i= 0; i != 4; ++i ) {
      samples[i]= analogRead( IR_IN );
  }
}

void share_data( ) {
  for( int i=0; i != 4; ++i ) {
    Serial.print( samples[i], DEC );
    Serial.print( "\t" );
  }
  Serial.println( );
}
```

[135]

Data Collection Gadgets

We defined a function to gather data and a function to share this data. We've broken the two features into separate functions so that we can easily tweak these as we go forward. We defined a buffer with room for four samples. This is an entirely arbitrary amount of data. It seems like enough to demonstrate the device is working. We can easily tweak this to be 16 samples, if we want to see more information.

This sketch introduces the `for` statement. This statement contains three clauses separated by `;` in the `()` and a body inside the `{}`:

- It has an initialization clause. We used `int i= 0` to create as well as initialize the integer variable `i`. This variable is local to the body of the `for` statement.

- It has a completion clause. We used `i != 4` so that we'll process the body of the `for` statement while the `i` variable is not equal to four, and stop when `i` is equal to four.

- It has an increment clause. We used `++i` to increment the value of the `i` variable by 1. We generally avoid the `++` operator in other contexts because the semantics can become confusing. In this context, however, there's no ambiguity.

These `for` statements are similar to Python's `for i in range(4)`. The three explicit clauses allow us to write very complex processing.

We shared the data by writing on the Arduino serial interface. We used the `Serial` object's `print()` function to provide a decimal representation of the input value. The Arduino IDE can capture this data for us on our computer.

This requires a change in the `setup()` as well:

```
void setup() {
  pinMode( LED, OUTPUT );
  digitalWrite( LED, LOW );
  Serial.begin( 9600 );
}
```

We added a `Serial.begin()` to open the serial output port for writing. The 9600 parameter specifies part of the hardware configuration. We'll return to the meaning of the 9600 later.

The overall `loop()` function might look like this to simply gather data every 2 seconds:

```
void loop() {
    static unsigned long last= 0;
    unsigned long now = millis();
```

```
    if (now-last > 2000) {
      gather_data();
      share_data();
      last= now;
    }
    heartbeat();
  }
```

We'll check the clock. If it's been 2 seconds since the last data gathering, we'll collect four data points and emit those four points. We'll also keep the heartbeat function running so that we can see the LEDs blinking to show the status of our board.

We can see the output when we open the Serial Monitor window in the Arduino IDE. When we open this window, we'll see a trickle of numbers as we wave our hands in front of the sensor. Once we've determined that things work, we'll need to create a slightly more stable setup. We might point the sensor at a wall. If we do, we'll see output that looks like this:

```
273 274    273    280
231 231    234    232
```

This shows that even when things aren't moving around, there's a small amount of variability in the output from the IR distance sensor. Each burst of four numbers seems to be nearly similar. Perhaps if we create a more stable environment and use a few clamps to hold a white paper card in place at a fixed distance from the sensor, we might get more consistent results.

The data sheet for the GP2Y0A02YK0F sensor includes a timing chart that shows a delay of 30 to 50 ms before a stable distance can be read. After a lag of 5 ms, the device will emit a new measurement. The data sheet shows us that the device will have moments of instability in the output. There's a long period of time with a stable reading and a short period of time with an unstable reading.

If we collect simple counts of matching raw data values, we'll see that about 64 percent of the raw values are completely consistent. Up to 75 percent are ±1 from the most common value, or mode. For example, if the mode is 251, then the three values between 250 and 252 account for 75 percent of the data. The problem we face is recognizing whether or not the first sample we read is part of the stable readings or is a reading from the small period of instability that occurs every 38 or so milliseconds.

We're forced to compute the mode over a small period of time. Because the Arduino can read (and process) a value in about 200 microseconds, it can read as many as 40 values in 5 milliseconds. The most common value among these will be the current distance.

Data Collection Gadgets

Our goal is to identify a current stable reading and turn this number into a useful distance measurement. For that, we'll need to do some more precise calibration. We'll enhance this data collection sketch to gather a few more samples suitable for statistical analysis. We can combine our button and distance reader so that the board can emit a burst of measurements. This will allow us to gather data at different distances and derive the exact relationship between the input voltage and distance.

Collecting bulk data with the Arduino

First, we'll expand our IR sensor reading sketch to wait for the sensor to show a stable reading. We'll use this stable reading algorithm to gather a batch of 16 samples from the sensor. This will give us some data that we can use for calibration.

The expanded version of the `gather_data()` function includes three separate features. We've left them in a single function, but they can be decomposed if required to make the Arduino more responsive. Here are the global variables shared by `gather_data()` and `share_data()`:

```
unsigned long start_time, end_time;
int raw_reading;
#define MODE_LIMIT 6
int reading[MODE_LIMIT];
int count[MODE_LIMIT];

const int TIME_LIMIT = 5000; // Microseconds.
```

We defined three important features for our data collection: the start time for reading, the end time for reading, and the raw value that was read. We included two other pieces of data definition that are unique to the Arduino language.

The `#define` statement creates a symbol that's used to modify the source prior to compiling it. In this case, `MODE_LIMIT` has a simple value of 6. Wherever `MODE_LIMIT` is used, a simple textual substitution is done to replace this with its replacement text of 6. If we change this value, the source text is changed in several places.

The values for `reading` and `count` are analogous to Python list structures. In Arduino, we'll call them arrays. They have an important difference from Python lists: arrays are of a fixed size. The size is defined when the sketch is compiled and cannot be changed without recompiling and uploading the sketch. The size, `MODE_LIMIT`, must be an integer constant. Because `#define` names do simple text substitution, this use of a symbol instead of a constant can be a handy clarification. It's better to see a consistent symbolic name than the number 6.

[138]

Chapter 5

We included a comment on the `TIME_LIMIT` variable to clarify the units. We don't mind waiting for 5,000 microseconds, that's only 5 milliseconds. We wouldn't want to wait 5,000 milliseconds. That would be 5 seconds.

Here's the first part of the `gather_data()` function:

```
// Read IR data computing a mode of no more than 16 distinct values.
// After TIME_LIMIT microseconds, return the mode.
void gather_data() {
  // Start gathering.
  start_time= micros();
  for( int i= 0; i != MODE_LIMIT; ++i ) { reading[i]= -1; count[i]= 0;
}
  // Next Sample. This could be a separate function, part of loop()
  while( micros()-start_time < TIME_LIMIT ) {
    int next= analogRead( IR_IN );
    for( int i= 0; i != MODE_LIMIT; ++i ) {
      if( reading[i] == next ) {
        count[i] += 1;
        break;
      }
      else if( reading[i] == -1 ) {
        reading[i] = next;
        break;
      }
    }
  }
}
```

We saved the starting time for our data gathering. We used a `for` statement to set all of the values in the `reading` to -1 and all the values of the `count` array to 0. We'll use the value -1 as a kind of sentinel to locate unused slots in the reading array. In Python, we'd append to the end of a list. In Arduino, we can't expand an array, so we'll use sentinel values instead.

We used the `while` statement to execute a sequence of statements while a given condition is true. In this case, we're subtracting the `start_time` value from the current time, given by `micros()`. If this is less than the value of `TIME_LIMIT`, we can continue gathering data to compute the mode. If this is false, we've run out of time, and we'll move to the rest of the `gather_data()` function.

Data Collection Gadgets

We'll use the `analogRead()` function to get another value from the IR device; we'll assign this to the `next` variable. Then, we'll use a `for` statement to examine each value in our array of readings:

- If the value in the `reading` array matches the value in `next`, we'll increment the matching value in the `count` array and break from the `for` statement.

- If the reading is -1, this is a sentinel. No previous value has matched, so we'll replace the value in the `reading` array with the value in `next`. We'll also break from the `for` statement.

- If we don't find a matching reading or a sentinel value, then the array of readings is full. Based on analysis of captured data, this is rare for an array with six positions in it. We'll wind up ignoring this value of `next`.

Once we've reached the time limit, we'll digest the frequency counts we've accumulated. Here's the rest of the `gather_data()` function:

```
// End processing
int mx = 0;
for( int i= 1; i != MODE_LIMIT; ++i ) {
  if( reading[i] == -1 ) break;
  if( count[i] > count[mx] ) mx= i;
}
raw_reading= reading[mx];
end_time= micros();
}
```

We initialized a local variable, `mx`, to zero. This is the value that is assumed to be the largest value in the `count` array. We'll use a `for` statement to compare the remaining values with this initial assumption. If any element of the count array is larger the value in `count[mx]`, we'll change `mx` to reflect this correction to our initial assumption. After examining all values, the value of `count[mx]` will be the largest count and the value of `reading[mx]` will be the most common reading.

Controlling data collection

The `share_data()` function needs to be expanded to emit the value of `raw_reading` instead of four samples. For deeper analysis (and debugging purposes), we'll want to update `share_data()` to print `start_time`, `end_time`, and the values from the `reading` and `count` arrays onto the serial interface.

We can then modify the main `loop()` to include the following:

```
void loop() {
    unsigned long push= debounce();
```

```
        if( push > 10 ) {
            for( int i= 0; i != 16; ++i ) {
                gather_data();
                share_data();
            }
        }
        heartbeat();
    }
```

This allows us to position a card at a known distance from the sensor and push the button. A little burst of data from the sensor will be sent through the serial interface. We can then move the card and gather another burst of data.

Data modeling and analysis with Python

We will use the `pyserial` module to write a separate data gathering application in Python. For this to work, we'll have to shut down the Arduino IDE so that our Python program can access the USB serial port.

A serial interface will see a stream of individual bits that can be reassembled into bytes. The low-level sequence of signals flips between high and low voltage at a defined rate, called baud. In addition to the baud, there are a number of other parameters that define serial interface configuration.

In some contexts, we might summarize an interface configuration as 9600/8-N-1. This says that we will exchange bits at 9600 baud, using 8-bit bytes, no parity checking, and a single stop bit included after the data bits. 8-N-1 specification after the "/" is a widely-used default and can be safely assumed. The transmission speed of 9600 baud can't be assumed, and needs to be stated explicitly. Our Arduino `Serial.begin(9600)` in the `setup()` function specified 9600 baud; this means that our Python data collection application must also specify 9600 baud. The Arduino default configuration is `SERIAL_8N1`, as is the `pyserial` default.

Even though flow control isn't used by default in the Arduino, it's best to always use a timeout option in our Python software. If the Arduino stops sending (or receiving), our Python application can continue operating. This means that we'll observe an empty line of input when there's no input available at the end of the timeout interval. We can ignore these empty lines and process everything else normally.

Data Collection Gadgets

Collecting data from the serial port

On Mac OS X, the OS representation of the serial port device is created when a physical device is plugged into a USB interface. We'll see the physical device appear as a name in the filesystem that looks like this: /dev/cu.*. To see this, use the OS command ls dev/cu.* before and after connecting the Arduino. On Windows, the behavior may be somewhat different, since the Windows COM0: and COM1: ports may exist without a device connected.

When the Arduino IDE is running, it will open the serial interface so that sketches can be uploaded. Since a Mac OS X or Linux serial device is used exclusively by a single process, we can't capture data from a Python application while the Arduino IDE is running. Once we've uploaded our sketch, we no longer need the Arduino IDE, and we can safely quit.

Once the Arduino IDE has stopped, we can use Python to read (and write) to the serial interface. If we forget to quit the Arduino IDE, we'll see exceptions when we try to connect to the serial interface in Python.

To communicate with the Arduino, we'll use serial.Serial to create a file that we can use for input or output. The basic connection looks like this:

```
import serial
import sys
def sample(port, baud=9600, limit=128):
    with serial.Serial(port, baud, timeout=1) as ir_sensor:
        while limit != 0:
            line= ir_sensor.readline()
            if line:
                print( line.decode("ascii").rstrip() )
                sys.stdout.flush()
                limit -= 1
```

We imported the serial module, which allows us to access USB serial devices from Python. We also imported the sys module so that we can work with sys.stdout. Our sample() function will gather up to 128 lines of input from the Arduino. This function opens the named serial interface device, usually "/dev/cu.usbmodem1421". We provided the ability to change the baud setting; since 9600 is a common default, we've made this a default for the baud parameter.

The timeout value of 1 means that the interface will wait for only 1 second for a complete line of input. If a complete line isn't available, the serial interface readline() method will return a zero-length string of bytes, b''. If a complete line (including the b'\r\n' at the end) is available, this string of bytes will be returned.

Chapter 5

The timeout is essential to prevent the interface from becoming stuck while it waits for the Arduino to provide input.

In order to show results as they become available, we included `sys.stdout.flush()`. This will assure that the output is displayed on the Python console as soon as it's available. This isn't essential, but it's a handy debugging feature. We often want immediate feedback that everything is working. We may have Python errors, Arduino sketch errors, or wiring problems. Using the `heartbeat()` function in our Arduino sketch and `sys.stdout.flush()` in our Python gives us a way to assess the root cause of a problem.

Formatting the collected data

The raw serial output—punctuated with `'\t'` characters—is directly useful in Python. We can use the `csv` module to parse this data. We can open a reader using `csv.reader(ir_sensor, delimiter='\t')` to properly split the columns.

For long-term analysis, it's useful to save data into a CSV file using a more common delimiter of `","`. It's also helpful to include a header row so that we know the meaning of the various integers in the file.

For calibration purposes, we'll want to use the expected distance and actual Arduino analog input values together as a sequence of simple pairs. This will allow us to create statistical models that correlate expected distance readings with input values.

Here's the Python side of our data collection. We'll show this as three functions. The first filters the Arduino data, discarding the line-ending characters as well as blank lines that happen when the serial interface times out:

```python
def gather(ir_sensor, samples=16):
    while samples != 0:
        line= ir_sensor.readline()
        if line:
            yield line.decode("ascii").rstrip()
            samples -= 1
```

This generator function will emit lines of sample data read from an Arduino. It requires that the serial interface has been opened properly and provided as the `ir_sensor` parameter. The upper limit on the number of samples has a default value of 16. This generator is a kind of filter that rejects empty lines. It's also a kind of map that converts bytes to proper Unicode characters.

Data Collection Gadgets

Each run of the experiment requires an expected distance value, collects data using the `gather()` function, and reformats it into a useful output. Here's a function that reformats the data from one experiment:

```python
import csv
def experiment_run(ir_sensor, writer, expected, samples=16):
    rdr= csv.reader(gather(ir_sensor, samples), delimiter='\t')
    for row in rdr:
        data = dict(
            Start= row[0],
            Stop= row[1],
            Raw= row[2],
            # Ignore 12 columns of measurement and count pairs.
            Expected= expected,
        )
        writer.writerow(data)
```

We provide this function the serial interface as the `ir_sensor` parameter, plus a CSV `DictWriter` object as the output. We also provided the value for the expected measurement to be added to each line of data and the number of samples to gather.

We used the `gather()` generator function to create a file-like iterable sequence of input lines. The `gather()` function rejects the blank lines which are an artifact of the timeout setting. We wrapped the output of `gather` with a `csv.reader()` that uses the `\t` delimiters to parse the columns of data.

We can then read each line of input from the serial interface, separate the raw and time values, and write the times, the raw value, and the expected distance to the output CSV file. This will give us a file of data that we can use for future analysis.

The overall main function prompts the user to enter an expected value. Once that's available, the user can press the data collection button on the Arduino to collect a batch of 16 samples.

```python
def collect_data():
    with serial.Serial(port, baud, timeout=1) as ir_sensor:
        with open("ir_data.csv", "w", newline="") as results:
            wtr= csv.DictWriter(results, ["Start", "Stop", "Raw",
"Expected"])
            wtr.writeheader()
            exp_str= input('Expected [q]: ')
            while not exp_str.lower().startswith('q'):
                try:
                    exp = int(exp_str)
                    distance_run(ir_sensor, wtr, exp)
```

```
        except ValueError as e:
            print(e)
        exp_str= input('Expected [q]: ')
```

This function will open the serial interface from the Arduino so that we can begin collecting data. It will also open a data collection file for the final data. We've used a `DictWriter` so that we'll have consistent headings on the file of collected data.

We've prompted an interactive user to enter an expected distance. If the user enters 'q' or even 'quit', we'll end the `while` statement, closing the two files. If the user enters a valid number for the expected distance, this will then collect 16 samples at the given expected distance using the `distance_run()` function.

The output will be a simple CSV file that looks like this:

```
Start,Stop,Raw,Expected
39248264,39253316,118,30
39255860,39260908,118,30
```

This shows the start time and end time for the data collection. These are in microseconds, and we expect the two times to be at least 5,000 microseconds apart from each other. The raw value also comes from the Arduino. The expected value was entered by the user and defines (in part) the experimental setup.

Crunching the numbers

Our calibration process works like this. First, we'll download the code to the Arduino. We can quit the Arduino IDE and start our Python data collection application. We enter a distance to our Python program and then stand up a paper card at a known distance from the sensor. When we push the data collection button on our prototype, the button's LED will flash as data is being collected. We can enter a new distance, move the card, push the button, and collect more data.

One of the first steps is to gather basic descriptive statistics on the raw data values in our CSV files. We'll generally use the mean and the standard deviation to compare two files of measurements. If we extract all the measurements at, for example, 15 cm distance, and the mean in one file is wildly different from the mean in another file, we can't simply lump the two files together. If the averages are not within three standard deviations of each other, the values are significantly different.

When we process these files, we'll make use of this handy function:

```
import csv
from types import SimpleNamespace
def nsreader(source):
    rdr= csv.DictReader(source)
```

Data Collection Gadgets

```
return (SimpleNamespace(**{k:int(v)
        for k,v in row.items()})
    for row in rdr)
```

This function works with the `csv` module to create a slightly easier-to-use data structure. The results of a `csv.DictReader` are a little awkward: we have to write `row['Raw']` to reference a specific column. In the case where all of the column names are valid Python identifiers, we can create a `SimpleNamespace` and use `row.Raw` to reference a specific column.

We used `{k:int(v) for k,v in row.items()}` to create a mapping from a key to an integer for each column in the source data. For our data gathering, this is convenient. In other contexts, we may have to develop a more sophisticated function to convert attributes to different data types.

The `SimpleNamespace(**{k:int(v) ... })` expression will use this mapping as the basis for creating the resulting `SimpleNamespace` object. Each key in this dictionary will become an attribute name. We wrapped this expression in a generator function so that we can iterate through the results of our `nsreader()` function.

We can use the `statistics` module to see the average, standard deviation, and variance for each collection of samples. We need to group the samples around the expected distance value that we recorded with each collection of 16 samples:

```python
from collections import defaultdict
from statistics import mean, stdev
def distance():
    by_dist = defaultdict(list)
    for filename in 'irdata_0.csv', 'irdata_1.csv', 'irdata_2.csv':
        with open(filename) as source:
            for row in nsreader(source):
                by_dist[row.Expected].append(row)

    for d in sorted(by_dist):
        m = mean( row.Raw for row in by_dist[d] )
        s = stdev( row.Raw for row in by_dist[d] )
        count = len(by_dist[d])
        print( "{d}cm n={count}: µ={m:7.3f}, "
                "σ={s:8.4f}".format_map(vars()) )
    print()
```

We created a `collections.defaultdict` that will contain lists of items that all have a common expected distance. We can then compare the 15 cm expected distance measurements from three calibration runs.

[146]

Once we've separated our data by expected distance, we can compute some descriptive statistics for each distance. In this case, we've used the `statistics` module to compute mean and standard deviation. The standard deviation is the square root of the variance: it also tells us how spread out the data is.

Here's some sample output:

```
irdata_0.csv
15cm n=16: μ=421.812, σ=   3.5444
20cm n=16: μ=254.438, σ=   2.9432
25cm n=16: μ=214.125, σ=   0.6191
```

We need to look at just the 15cm data for each run:

```
15cm n=16: μ=421.812, σ=   3.5444
15cm n=16: μ=299.438, σ=   2.3085
15cm n=16: μ=300.312, σ=   1.0145
```

Clearly, the first run isn't measuring the same thing the second and third runs are measuring. Something must have been different in that setup. The data is more variable and the average is remarkably different from the other two runs.

Over 90 percent of the data should fall within three standard deviations of a given mean. With a mean of about 300 and a standard deviation of about 2.3, we expect data to fall between 293 and 307. A mean of about 421 is very unlikely to belong to the same population.

Creating a linear model

The data sheet for most IR devices shows a kind of inverse power curve between voltage and distance. We've only measured the performance between 15 cm and 30 cm, which is a fraction of the overall range the device is capable of. One of the reasons for limiting the range is because this portion of the range appears linear. Another reason is that a 12-inch desk ruler only covers about 30 cm. A meter stick or yard stick would show different results.

We can—with a small transformation—convert the nonlinear power curve data to a proper power curve. We might, for example, use `1/raw` to convert the raw value in a way that leads to more accurate position calculation over a wider range of distances. This conversion is something we'll leave for agents who need more accuracy over greater distances. Our data is only measured over a short range of 15 cm to 30 cm and appears linear over that range.

[147]

Data Collection Gadgets

To create the conversion between reading and distance, we'll create a linear model. This will give us the two parameters for the equation $y = \beta x + a$. In this case, y is the linear distance, in cm, x is the input reading (ideally, as a voltage, but we'll see that the raw reading also works over short distances). β is the slope of the line, and a is the y-axis intercept where x equals zero.

The Python `statistics` module does not include a linear estimation function. A little search among sources on the internet turns up a number of approaches. We'll rely on the following calculations for the two coefficients.

$$\beta = r \times \frac{\sigma_y}{\sigma_x}$$

$$a = \mu_y - \beta \times \mu_x$$

The values for σ_x and σ_y are the standard deviations of x and y values. The values for μ_x and μ_y are the means of these two variables. The value for r is the Pearson correlation coefficient. We can calculate it as follows:

$$r = \frac{\sum z(x)_i \times z(y)_i}{(N-1)}$$

The value N is the number of samples. The values $z(x)_i$ and $z(y)_i$ are standardized z-scores computed from the value, the population mean, and the population standard deviation. We convert each raw value to the number of standard deviations from the mean:

$$z(x)_i = \frac{(x_i - \mu_x)}{\sigma_x}$$

$$z(y)_i = \frac{(y_i - \mu_y)}{\sigma_y}$$

We can implement this linear estimation as the following Python function:

```python
from statistics import mean, stdev, pstdev
def z( x, μ_x, σ_x ):
    return (x-μ_x)/σ_x
def linest( pairs ):
```

```python
x_seq = tuple(p[0] for p in pairs)
y_seq = tuple(p[1] for p in pairs)
μ_x, σ_x= mean(x_seq), stdev(x_seq)
μ_y, σ_y= mean(y_seq), stdev(y_seq)
z_x = (z(x, μ_x, σ_x) for x in x_seq)
z_y = (z(y, μ_y, σ_y) for y in y_seq)
r_xy = sum( zx*zy for zx, zy in zip(z_x, z_y) )/len(pairs)
beta= r_xy * σ_y/σ_x
alpha= μ_y - beta*μ_x
return r_xy, alpha, beta
```

We ensured the input to be a list of (x, y) pairs. We'll compute a model that predicts the y values from the x values. We decomposed the sequence of pairs into a sequence of x values and a sequence of y values. (This two-step process means that the `pairs` variable *must* be a sequence object, and it can't be an iterable generator of values.)

We calculate the mean and standard deviation values for both sequences. We also use two generator expressions to apply the `z()` function to create two sequences of standardized values from the original sequences of raw values. The `z()` function is so small that we could have used a lambda object: `z=lambda x, μ_x, σ_x: (x-μ_x)/σ_x`. This can be confusing, so we defined a complete, but small function.

Once we have the set of standardized z-values, we can compute the correlation between the two sequences, given by the `r_xy` variable. We use the construct `for zx, zy in zip(z_x, z_y)` to process matching values from the two parallel sequences. From the `r_xy` value, we compute the alpha and beta parameters of the linear model that maps x values to y values.

We can use a function like this to show the linear model:

```python
def correlation(filename, xform=lambda x:x):
    with open(filename) as source:
        data = nsreader(source)
        pairs = list( (xform(row.Raw), row.Expected) for row in data)
    r, alpha, beta = linest(pairs)
    r_2 = r*r
    print( "r² = {r_2:.4f}".format_map(vars()) )
    print( "d = {beta:.5f}*raw + {alpha:.2f}".format_map(vars()) )
```

This will extract the `Raw` and `Expected` attributes values from one of our collected data files. We used the `nsreader()` to create namespace objects, which allows us to use syntax like `row.Expected` to reference an attribute of a sample. We've applied the `xform` function to each `Raw` value. The default **xform** function is a lambda object which does nothing. We can supply different functions (or lambda objects) to explore any transformations that might be needed to make the raw data linear.

Data Collection Gadgets

We'll use the `pairs` list as the argument to the `linest()` function. This will return the correlation, r, plus the parameters for the linear model, `alpha` and `beta`. We compute the r^2 value because this shows the fraction of the variance that's explained by the linear model.

The output for the `ir_data.csv` file looks like this:

```
r² = 0.8267
d = -0.12588*raw + 43.90
```

This tells us that 82 percent of the values will be predicted by this formula. The actual formula for distance is given next. We can implement this in our Arduino and report actual distance instead of a raw voltage measurement. It's a small change to the sketch to do this additional distance calculation.

We've followed a multi-step procedure for calibrating our measurement and data collection device:

1. We ran some controlled experiments to gather data points.
2. We did some basic statistics to see what parts of the data were usable.
3. We created a linear model to describe the data.

We can then modify the software in our device based on this calibration procedure. This becomes part of an ongoing effort to gather and analyze raw data to be sure our device's results are meaningful.

Reducing noise with a simple filter

Is there a way that we can reduce the variability in the output? One possibility to use a moving average of the raw values. Using an Exponentially Weighted Moving Average (EWMA) algorithm will tend to damp out small perturbations in the data, providing a more stable reading.

This moving average is called exponentially weighted because the weights given to previous values fall off exponentially. The immediately previous value is weighted more heavily than the value before that. All values figure into the current value, but as we go back in time, the weights for those old values become very, very small.

The core calculation for a weighted data point, s_i, from the raw data point, r_i, looks like this:

$$s_i = w \times r_i + (1-w) \times s_{i-1}$$

We used a weighting value, w, that expresses the influence of the previous data point on the current data point. If w is one, previous values have no influence. If w is zero, the initial value is the only one that matters and new values are ignored.

The very first data point, s_0, can be simply the first raw point, r_0. No transformation is applied; this initial value is used to start the processing.
A common variation is to average an initial burst of four values.

A weighting value of $w = \dfrac{1}{3}$, for example, means that each new point consists of 1/3 of the next raw value and 2/3 of the all of the previously weighted values. This means that small variations will be ignored. As we move back in time, the effective weightings for those older and older values are 0.666, 0.444, 0.296, 0.197, etc.

We can explore the impact of this filter using the raw data we've already collected. We can write a function like this to experiment with different weighting values:

```
def ewma(row_iter, w=0.4):
    row = next(row_iter)
    r = row.Raw
    s = r
    row.Weighted = s
    yield row
    for row in row_iter:
        r= row.Raw
        s= round(w*r + (1-w)*s)
        row.Weighted= s
        yield row
```

This generator function will apply a weighting of w = 0.4 to the value of Raw in each item in the row_iter sequence of values. We use the next() function to extract the initial item, row, which we use to seed the raw values, r, and the sequence of weighted values, s. In this case, we seeded the weighted sequence with a single initial value. An alternative is to create an unweighted average of the first few values.

We inserted the weighted value into each row of data, setting the Weighted attribute of each row. We then yielded the modified row.

Data Collection Gadgets

For all of the remaining items in the `row_iter` sequence, we'll get the value of the `Raw` attribute, `r`. From this, we'll compute the weighted moving average, `s`. As with the first item, we'll insert this back into the row as the `Weighted` attribute and yield the modified row.

This is a mapping from the input data to an extended form of the input data. Interestingly, this kind of mapping is difficult to do with the built-in `map()` function. The transformation we're applying that creates the `Weighted` value from the `Raw` value is a stateful transformation: something a generator function does well.

As an initial experiment, we can look at the data like this:

```
from ch_5_ex_3 import nsreader
with open("irdata_2.csv") as data:
    for row in ewma(nsreader(data)):
        print(row.Raw, row.Weighted)
```

This small script allows us to see the effect of the `ewma()` generator function by comparing the `Raw` and `Weighted` values. We'll see sequences of data that shows the raw and weighted values:

```
300 300
299 300
301 300
```

The raw value jumped around between 299 and up to 301; the weighted value stayed steady at 300. Here's a second example of data from this weighted moving average:

```
300 300
301 300
300 300
288 295
288 292
289 291
```

In this case, the distance from the IR reader to the target jumped suddenly from 300 to 288 (from 15 cm to 16 cm). The weighted moving average stepped down slowly through 300, 295, 292, and 291. A good consequence of the weighted moving average is that small changes are damped out; a large change will be slowed down.

We can easily implement this algorithm in the Arduino. We can couple this with our linear model for translating the weighted value to a distance. This provides us with a slowly changing distance measure.

Chapter 5

Solving problems adding an audible alarm

We used LEDs to provide feedback. We started with a heartbeat LED that showed us that our sketch was running properly. We can easily add LEDs based on other conditions. For example, we might add red and green LEDs to show when the distance being measured is outside certain limits.

We'll need to add appropriate resistors for these LEDs. We'll also need to allocate two pins to control these LEDs.

We can convert the raw measurement into a distance with a simple calculation in the Arduino program. We might add code somewhat like this:

```
float next = debounce_ir();
float raw = next*w + (1-w)*current;
float d = -0.12588*raw + 43.90;
```

This depends on a `debounce_ir()` function that reads a single distance value from the IR device. This is a small change to our `gather_data()` function. We want to return a value instead of update a global variable.

We used a EWMA algorithm to compute the weighted moving average of the sequence of raw values. This is saved in a global variable, `raw`. It depends on a weighting value, `w`, which we developed by exploring the data with a Python program. We then converted this to a distance value, `d`, which we can use for illuminating some LEDs.

We can then use this distance value in `if` statements:

```
if( d < 16.0 ) { digitalWrite( RED_LED, HIGH ); }
else { digitalWrite( RED_LED, LOW );   }
if( d > 29.0 ) { digitalWrite( GREEN_LED, HIGH ); }
else { digitalWrite( GREED_LED, LOW );   }
```

This requires us to define the two pins used for the red and green limit LEDs. We can experiment with this to be sure that LEDs goes on when a target is placed too close or too far from the sensor.

We can also add a Piezo speaker and use the Arduino `tone()` and `noTone()` functions to create audible signals. Note that the speaker requires a small resistor, usually 100 Ω, to reduce the voltage to a manageable level.

[153]

Data Collection Gadgets

Instead of setting a pin to `HIGH` or `LOW`, we use the `tone()` function to provide a frequency (try 1,000) and a duration (1,000 milliseconds or 1 second). This will produce a handy beep noise that serves as an audio alert.

When starting out on this kind of mission, it's hard to know where we'll end up. A single alarm LED or two LEDs as the limits are being reached? A tone? Multiple tones? The exact feedback we need is difficult to imagine without seeing the device in operation. Being able to change the device easily allows us to experiment with different kinds of interactions.

Summary

In this chapter, we looked at data collection at the gadget level. We used an Arduino board to build a data collection gadget. We looked at how we can build a simple display using LEDs. We also discussed providing simple input by debouncing a push button. We used Python programs to help us design some of these circuits.

We also used the analog input pins to gather data from an infrared distance sensor. To be sure that we've got reliable, usable data, we wrote a calibration process. We collected that raw data and analyzed it in Python. Because of the sophisticated `statistics` module, we were able to evaluate the quality of the results.

We used Python to build a linear model that maps the raw measurements to accurate distance measurements. We can use these Python analytical modules for ongoing calibration and fine-tuning the way this device works.

We also used Python to examine the parameters for an EWMA algorithm. We can use Python to explore the weighting factor. It's very easy to process raw data from the Arduino device and tweak the Python algorithms quickly and easily. Once we arrived at a good algorithm, we can implement it in the Arduino.

We built a device that becomes part of the Internet of Things (IoT.) This small device produces a stream of serial data that a computer can capture and process. With a foundation of data gathering, transformation, and upload, we're able to create additional gadgets that work with different kinds of data.

In our first missions, we upgraded and extended Python to add state-of-the-art modules and components. This is a regular practice that all agents need to follow. The pace of change is supplied in documents available at `https://www.python.org/dev/peps/pep-0429/`. This information helps us keep current with the ever-changing world of open source software.

[154]

Chapter 5

One of the common types of mission involves extracting or analyzing data from log files. Many pieces of software, including databases and web servers, keep extensive logs. Anyone who creates a web site has access to the logs that show what parts of the site are being accessed. This data is voluminous, and Python tools are one common way to digest and summarize the details.

One of the most useful sources of information is other people. We can connect with other people through the numerous social networks that people join. There are in-person groups that we can find using sites like `http://www.meetup.com`. We can search for like-minded groups using keywords like Python, Arduino, or Maker.

We can also use online social networks to locate people, and their interests. Some social network web sites, such as `https://twitter.com` have very sophisticated Application Program Interfaces (API). We can often find the kind of information we want using Twitter's very sophisticated API. Other social network web sites aren't quite so sophisticated, and we may be forced to do more work to analyze and interpret the data.

In some cases, we're forced to work with data sources that aren't simple to analyze. A PDF file, for example, might have a great deal of useful information, but it may also be difficult to parse. We've looked at one (of many) libraries that attempt to do a useful decoding of PDF content. The `pdfminer` package seems to provide a useful level of flexibility for extracting data that might be otherwise locked into a PDF.

Our final missions showed us how we can use the Internet of Things to gather data. The common theme that many agents observe is that raw data isn't as useful as data that's properly analyzed and summarized. Merely collecting bits and bytes of data isn't what HQ needs. The truly successful agents transform raw data into actionable information.

Index

A

analog data
collecting 135-137
Apache CLF
URL 44
Apache logs
URL 35
Arduino
bulk data, collecting with 138-140
defining 116, 117
flexible and responsive, to
fluid situation 118, 119
references 116
shopping list, organizing 118
Arduino IDE
obtaining 29, 30
URL 29
Arduino programming language
arithmetic operators, using 127, 128
common processing statements,
using 128, 129
comparison operators, using 127, 128
Edit-Compile-Test-Break cycle,
defining 130
mastering 126, 127
Arduino sensor data feed 132-134

B

Beautiful Soup
HTML page, obtaining 21
HTML structure, navigating 22-24
reference 20
upgrading 20

blinking light 130, 131
blocks of text
displaying 101-103
bulk data
collecting, with Arduino 138-140
Busy Waiting design 132

C

CadSoft
about 116
URL 116
collected data
formatting 143-145
Common Log Format (CLF)
about 34
definition 44
fields 45
pattern 46
complex layouts
defining 103-105
content filter
writing 105, 106
cooked strings
versus raw strings 39
CSV output
emitting 111, 112

D

data
collecting, from serial port 142
scraping, from PDF files 26, 27
data collection
controlling 140

data modeling and analysis
with Python 141
design principles, for methods 99
digital output pins
external LED, designing 121-123
starting with 119, 120
working prototype, assembling 124-126
diode 121
document
text data, obtaining from 100, 101
downloads
tracking 52, 53

E

EARTH character 14
entities
about 75
URL 75
Expandable Cloud Computing (EC2) 35

F

filter
noise, reducing with 150-152
Flickr
URL, for photos 66
Fritzing application
URL 31
Fritzing tool
URL 31
ftplib
solution, for obtaining logs from server 62

G

gadgets
building 28, 29
generator expressions
Eager 90
Lazy 91
Google Cloud Platform
URL 73
grid
exposing 108, 109
gzip compressed file
reading 48, 49

H

http client
web services, accessing with 68-71
Hypertext Transfer Protocol (HTTP) 68

I

image processing
with PIL package 66, 67

J

JavaScript Object Notation (JSON) 24, 34

L

language analysis 83, 84
Latin America or Caribbean (LAC) 57
linear model
creating 147-149

N

Network Information Center (NIC) 57
NLTK
about 83, 84
reference link 85
noise
reducing, with simple filter 150-152
numbers
defining 145, 146

O

Optical Character Recognition (OCR) 87
other upgrades
defining 24

P

page iterator
filtering 107
PDF content
bad data, filtering 93, 94
context manager, writing 94, 95
extracting 90
generator expressions, using 90, 91

generator functions, writing 92
PDF parser resource
   manager, writing 96, 97
resource manager, extending 97-100
PDF document
about 90
URL 90
PDF files
data, scraping from 26, 27
PDF Miner
references 90
PDF Miner 3k
URL 26
pdf package
URL 26
PDFPageInterpreter 90
PDFParser 90
PDFResourceManager 90
Pillow
references 24
PIL package
used, for processing image 66, 67
pip application
using 20
ply package
defining 28
references 27
Portable Document Format (PDF)
defining 88, 89
URL 89
PostScript 89
PyPI
URL 20
PySerial
URL 31
Python
about 28
URL 3
used, for running other programs 56, 57
Python 3 compatibility
URL 20
Python Enhancement Proposals (PEP)
about 2
URL 2
Python language
data, comparing 13, 14
dictionary mapping, using 12, 13

for statement, using 16
functions, defining 17, 18
if statement, using 15
logic operators, using 13, 14
reviewing 6, 7
script files, creating 18, 19
simple statements, using 14
strings, using 8-10
tuples and lists, using 11, 12
variables used, for saving results 7, 8
while statement, using 16
Python serial interface
obtaining 31

R

raw data
Conceptual Content 47
gzip compressed file, reading 48, 49
Logical Layout 47
Physical Format 47
reading 47
raw strings
versus cooked strings 39
Read Eval Print Loop (REPL) 6
regular expression
characters, capturing by name 43, 44
CLF 44-46
pattern, searching in file 38-41
rules and patterns 37, 38
suffix operators, using 41-43
writing, for parsing 35-37
Regular Expression Strings 37
remote files
reading 50
Representational State Transfer (REST) 34
resistors
adding, for LEDs 153, 154
RFC 3912
URL 58

S

semiconductor 121
Spinning 130
suffix operators
using 41-43

T

tables
defining 103-105
text block recognition tweaks
creating 110
text data
obtaining, from document 100, 101
toolkit
expanding 25, 26
tools
defining 2
features 2
housecleaning 2
performance 2
pip, upgrading 5, 6
Python, upgrading 3-5
reasons 2
security 2
Twitter API project, on PyPI
URL 25
Twitter social network
conversation, examining 79-81
followers, searching 76-79
images being posted, gathering 81-83
profile information, obtaining 74-76
URL 74
user information, gathering 71-73

U

urllib
web services, accessing with 68-71

W

weather forecasts
URL 21
web server logs
formats 35
obtaining 35
obtaining, from server with ftplib 61, 62
overview 34
studying 50, 51
web services
accessing, with http client 68-71
accessing, with urllib 68-71
Whois program
about 34, 55, 56
bulk requests, creating 60
Python, using 56, 57
reference link 55
request, decomposing 58, 59
stanza-finding algorithm 60
URL 55
whois queries, processing 57, 58
World Wide Web (WWW) 68

Y

Yacc (Yet Another Compiler Compiler) 28

Thank you for buying
Python for Secret Agents
Volume II

About Packt Publishing
Packt, pronounced 'packed', published its first book, *Mastering phpMyAdmin for Effective MySQL Management*, in April 2004, and subsequently continued to specialize in publishing highly focused books on specific technologies and solutions.

Our books and publications share the experiences of your fellow IT professionals in adapting and customizing today's systems, applications, and frameworks. Our solution-based books give you the knowledge and power to customize the software and technologies you're using to get the job done. Packt books are more specific and less general than the IT books you have seen in the past. Our unique business model allows us to bring you more focused information, giving you more of what you need to know, and less of what you don't.

Packt is a modern yet unique publishing company that focuses on producing quality, cutting-edge books for communities of developers, administrators, and newbies alike. For more information, please visit our website at www.packtpub.com.

About Packt Open Source
In 2010, Packt launched two new brands, Packt Open Source and Packt Enterprise, in order to continue its focus on specialization. This book is part of the Packt Open Source brand, home to books published on software built around open source licenses, and offering information to anybody from advanced developers to budding web designers. The Open Source brand also runs Packt's Open Source Royalty Scheme, by which Packt gives a royalty to each open source project about whose software a book is sold.

Writing for Packt
We welcome all inquiries from people who are interested in authoring. Book proposals should be sent to author@packtpub.com. If your book idea is still at an early stage and you would like to discuss it first before writing a formal book proposal, then please contact us; one of our commissioning editors will get in touch with you.

We're not just looking for published authors; if you have strong technical skills but no writing experience, our experienced editors can help you develop a writing career, or simply get some additional reward for your expertise.

OpenCV for Secret Agents

ISBN: 978-1-78328-737-6   Paperback: 302 pages

Use OpenCV in six secret projects to augment your home, car, phone, eyesight, and any photo or drawing

1. Build OpenCV apps for the desktop, the Raspberry Pi, Android, and the Unity game engine.

2. Learn real-time techniques that can be used to classify images, detecting and recognizing any person or animal, and studying motion and distance with superhuman precision.

3. Design hands-free interfaces that are practical in home automation, in cars, and in discrete surveillance.

BeagleBone for Secret Agents

ISBN: 978-1-78398-604-0   Paperback: 162 pages

Browse anonymously, communicate secretly, and create custom security solutions with open source software, the BeagleBone Black, and cryptographic hardware

1. Interface with cryptographic hardware to add security to your embedded project, securing you from external threats.

2. Use and build applications with trusted anonymity and security software like Tor and GPG to defend your privacy and confidentiality.

3. Work with low level I/O on BeagleBone Black like I2C, GPIO, and serial interfaces to create custom hardware applications.

Please check **www.PacktPub.com** for information on our titles

Learning OpenCV 3 Computer Vision with Python
Second Edition

ISBN: 978-1-78528-384-0   Paperback: 266 pages

Unleash the power of computer vision with Python using OpenCV

1. Create impressive applications with OpenCV and Python.

2. Familiarize yourself with advanced machine learning concepts.

3. Harness the power of computer vision with this easy-to-follow guide.

Learning Penetration Testing with Python

ISBN: 978-1-78528-232-4   Paperback: 314 pages

Utilize Python scripting to execute effective and efficient penetration tests

1. Understand how and where Python scripts meet the need for penetration testing.

2. Familiarise yourself with the process of highlighting a specific methodology to exploit an environment to fetch critical data.

3. Develop your Python and penetration testing skills with real-world examples.

Please check **www.PacktPub.com** for information on our titles

Made in the USA
Lexington, KY
15 March 2019